# THE EVOLUTION OF
# THE SIX-FOUR CHORD

Da Capo Press Music Reprint Series

GENERAL EDITOR
FREDERICK FREEDMAN
VASSAR COLLEGE

# THE EVOLUTION OF
# THE SIX-FOUR CHORD

## *A Chapter in the History of*
## *Dissonance Treatment*

BY

GLEN HAYDON

———

WITH AN INTRODUCTION

BY

ALBERT I. ELKUS

𝄢 DA CAPO PRESS · NEW YORK · 1970

A Da Capo Press Reprint Edition

This Da Capo Press edition of
*The Evolution of the Six-Four Chord*
is an unabridged republication of the first edition
published in Berkeley, California, in 1933.

Library of Congress Catalog Card Number 75-125052
SBN 306-70017-4

Published by Da Capo Press
A Division of Plenum Publishing Corporation
227 West 17th Street, New York, N.Y. 10011

Manufactured in the United States of America

# THE EVOLUTION OF
# THE SIX-FOUR CHORD

*A Chapter in the History of*
*Dissonance Treatment*

# THE EVOLUTION OF
# THE SIX-FOUR CHORD

*A Chapter in the History of
Dissonance Treatment*

BY

GLEN HAYDON

———

WITH AN INTRODUCTION
BY
ALBERT I. ELKUS

UNIVERSITY OF CALIFORNIA PRESS
BERKELEY, CALIFORNIA
1933

SALES REPRESENTATIVES:

UNIVERSITY OF CALIFORNIA PRESS
BERKELEY, CALIFORNIA

———

CAMBRIDGE UNIVERSITY PRESS
LONDON, ENGLAND
*For orders originating in Great Britain only*

PRINTED IN THE UNITED STATES OF AMERICA

TO
KNUD JEPPESEN

# CONTENTS

# INTRODUCTION

D R. HAYDON'S TREATISE on *The Evolution of the Six-four Chord* is a welcome contribution to the study of a period of music which has long been revered but little
understood.

The six-four chord is a dissonance which is characteristic both of the contrapuntal
and the harmonic school and forms a connecting link between them. Very early it
claimed its place in music. Its development is no doubt similar to that of many, if not
all, dissonant chords; first the instinctive and sometimes even crude use of a dissonance
for its own sake and later its crystallization into a chord, not necessarily because of any
basic affinity existing between its tones, but on account of its use and function. The
same process is at work with regard to dissonance in contemporary music. Indeed, the
history of all of our dissonances suggests that a chord should be defined as any group of
tones which have become convincingly associated.

In its earlier uses, the fourth in combination with the sixth appears in many
formulae, and it is interesting to follow the various instinctive approaches of composers
and musicians who had very little idea of what they were accomplishing harmonically.
As contrapuntal music develops, the formulae become fewer, so that at the height of
the Italian Church school only the strongest and most poignant are commonly found.
The tendency is away from variety and diffuseness toward simplicity and strength.

With the discarding of the many for the fewer formulae, the dissonance tends to
increase by contrast the effect of consonance; but the reverse is also true—it is the
surrounding and contrasting consonance that increases the effect of the dissonance.
There is little doubt—and the present research confirms this view—that in every
stage of music, dissonance has been employed for its own sake, and the restrictions
which have invariably arisen to govern its use (resolution, preparation, etc.) have often
tended to throw it into stronger relief.

Apparently each period of music starts with an instinctive and adventuresome use
of dissonance. In its culmination it develops a technique which, while narrowing the
limits of the application of dissonance, intensifies its effect. This very intensification of
effect by a self-imposed and orderly technique is perhaps characteristic of classic periods
in art, and one of the most suggestive points in this treatise is that showing the direction
of the development of the chord from its diffuse and freer use by the primitives to its
reserved and concentrated use in the Palestrina period. To appreciate this properly, the
reader should refer to Dr. Jeppesen's research on *The Style of Palestrina and the Dissonance*,[1] to which, in certain respects, Dr. Haydon's treatise is a complementary study.

Interesting, furthermore, is the reciprocal play of influence which appears to have
existed between this chord and the development of the major and minor system of
tonality. This is best illustrated in the English Madrigal School. Here the chord is to
be found on various degrees of the scale, particularly the fourth and sixth degrees. In
producing its characteristic cadential effect, it suggests, or actually brings about, a
modulation. Thus the chord, the product of a contrapuntally-minded period, exerts a

---

[1] Translated into English by Margaret W. Hamerick (Oxford Univ. Press, 1927).

strong influence in developing the harmonic aspect of music. For this privilege, however, it pays a penalty. On account of its tendency to stabilize tonality, its use becomes more limited and conventional.

This most interesting treatise leaves me with a sense of intimacy with the six-four chord. Knowing of its early struggles and triumphs, and bearing in mind certain of its uses in recent music, I find myself wishing it a long life and new adventures.

ALBERT I. ELKUS

University of California
February, 1933

# PREFACE

THE SIX-FOUR CHORD has long been the subject of animated discussion and careful thought. Many theories have been expounded, elaborated, and presented on the origin, nature, development, use, characteristics, and qualities of this combination. The average textbook on Harmony explains it as being the second inversion of a primary triad which, however, because of the dissonant character of the fourth occurring in this position of the triad, must be handled with a certain discretion such as is necessary with all dissonant combinations in musical composition. For the most part the rules given for the treatment of this chord are derived from the rules stated in the theory books of the preceding generation, modified and amplified by the consideration of the actual use of the chord by the composers of the particular period in which the work is written. The average Counterpoint textbook takes a very skeptical attitude toward the six-four chord and often considers it too much of a purely harmonic device to be suitable material for use in contrapuntal study. A consideration of all the various points of view would in itself provide material for a separate study.

Wilhelm Rischbieter[1] writes in his introduction:

We find, to be sure, in certain practical Harmony textbooks very good rules regarding the use of this chord —$\binom{6}{4}$—, but up to the present time a scientific basis for these rules is lacking. This probably accounts for the fact that the rules laid down for the treatment of this chord are so varied. In the two following essays I have made the attempt to show the natural laws governing modulation and the use of the six-four chord.

As the title of his book suggests, his treatment is from a theoretical viewpoint and he makes no attempt to discuss the six-four chord in the light of its historical development in the works of the masters.

The difficulty in the treatment of the six-four chord arises from the fact that the physicists consider the intervals of the fourth and sixth as consonances[2] and also the corresponding six-four chord,[3] whereas in the realms of theoretical and applied music and of Physiology, Psychology, etc., the fourth,[4] especially above the bass (as has already been stated), and therefore also the six-four chord, have commonly been treated as if each were a dissonance.

G. Capellen writes:[5]

The peculiar nature of the six-four chord has caused the theorists of all periods a great deal of difficulty. In spite of the manifold discussions in the textbooks, and in spite of the monograph of Rischbieter, the problem of this chord still remains unsolved from a scientific standpoint, because the customary empirically established rules have only a casuistic value and unified points of view which may be applicable to all cases are lacking, as the following selections from the views of the theorists will show: . . . .

---

[1] *Drei theoretische Abhandlungen über Modulation, Quartsextakkord und Orgelpunkt* (Dresden, 1879), pp. 5 and 6.

[2] Schaefer, K. L., *Musikalische Akustik* (Berlin, 1923), p. 121, says: "Die dem gegenwärtigen allgemeinen Urteile am besten entsprechende Stufenfolge der Konsonanzen dürfte diese sein: Oktave, Quinte und Quarte, grosse Terz und grosse Sexte, kleine Terz und kleine Sexte."

[3] See for example A. Kalähne in Müller-Pouillet, *Lehrbuch der Physik* (Braunschweig, 1929), vol. 1, pt. 3, "Akustik," pp. 119, 126–127. Kalähne evolves both the major six-four chord and the minor six-four chord as consonant.

[4] And in certain relations the sixth, too, has been considered as dissonant ("Auffassungs-Dissonanz")—see Louis, R., und Thuille, L., *Harmonielehre* (Stuttgart, 1913), pp. 46 ff.

[5] "Der Quartsextakkord," SIMG, 3: 167.

Capellen then quotes passages from a number of theorists and sums up the problem in the following words:[6]

It will be seen that the problem hinges on the following questions: (*a*) Is the fourth in the six-four chord a consonance or a dissonance? (*b*) Is the (accented) six-four chord an independent or decorative chord [appoggiatura or suspension]? (*c*) What is the relation of the six-four chord to the tonality?

Although he states that in order to be able to answer these questions it is necessary to investigate and determine how the six-four chord occurs "in der Praxis," his own work does not undertake such a research.

R. Münnich,[7] writing of concords and discords says, after pointing out some of the difficulties in connection with the classification of the six-four chord:

I believe, therefore, that inclusion of the separate chords under the categories "consonance" and "dissonance" is a task which can only be accomplished if one looks up the chords in the practical literature itself and then carefully examines and tests the numerous factors which have an influence on the conception of the structure; and finally, [thus] progressing from case to case on the basis of a careful and clear analysis, [one] reaches a decision. Unfortunately we have no such monographs which systematically hunt up the chords in their contexts in the works of the masters and thus provide, once and for all, objective factual material. *This is the point at which a beginning must be made*[8] if we want to press on beyond the treatment of the most elementary and general theoretical problems to the mastery of the internal harmonic problems and to the building up of a system of Harmony which is scientifically grounded in all its parts.

The initial impulse to the writing of the present treatise, however, is to be found in a much more general problem than the treatment of the six-four chord as such, and that is—the whole subject of the treatment of the dissonance. Jeppesen[9] speaks of his work as being "a preliminary treatise upon the history of dissonance treatment." He gives a clear-cut and excellent statement of the problem; of the difficulties to be overcome in the lack of source material; of the beginnings made by Ambros and Riemann; of the infrequency of attempts "to regard matters in their historic continuity"; and of the frequent divergencies between musical theory and musical technique as actually displayed in the compositions themselves. Jeppesen states the reasons for these differences as follows:

(1) An inclination that is common to these writers [the theorists] to theorize on their own account (speculative methods, exaggerated tendency to systematize).

(2) The moment of inertia which causes the theorist to transfer rules from older textbooks to new without proper critical revision, and without first ascertaining if these rules were in force during the period under discussion.

(3) Inability of the theorists, when describing the practices of past times, to discriminate between these and the elements of style typical of their own contemporaries (which was the case with Fux).

(4) Pedagogic considerations, which often tend to a simplification or rounding-off of the set of rules belonging to the style, or likewise sometimes a stricter rendering of these rules—for the sake of exercise.

All this does not, however, as Jeppesen points out, keep the musical theorist, considered with due critical insight, from giving valuable service in the field of musical history, etc.

---

[6] *Op. cit.*, p. 168.    [7] "Konkordanz und Diskordanz," ZIMG, 13: 55.    [8] Italics by author of present work.
[9] *The Style of Palestrina and the Dissonance* (Leipzig, 1925; Eng. tr., London, Oxford Univ. Press, 1927), p. 1.

The whole history of dissonance is, naturally, too large a subject to be thoroughly dealt with in all its ramifications and implications in a single treatise. In order to bring the whole subject within practical workable bounds, there must first be a series of separate limited investigations; ultimately, it may then be possible to write a comprehensive statement of the whole subject based on the results of these preliminary findings. There are at least two obvious methods of procedure, each of which has its own peculiar advantages and disadvantages, namely:

(1) The works of one composer can be examined and analyzed with respect to his treatment of all types of dissonance.

(2) A certain type of dissonance can be traced as it reappears in the works of composers of successive periods.

Jeppesen, for reasons which he has stated,[10] has chosen the former method with the work of Palestrina as his first field of investigation. The author of the present treatise has chosen the latter method with the six-four chord as the subject of his initial research because of the peculiar possibilities which it offers for presenting and explaining the subject clearly and thoroughly, while at the same time recording the story of its evolution.

As Jeppesen suggests, speaking of the dissonance in general, if we should

begin the experiment with the first polyphonic period, advancing therefrom to Palestrina, we should soon become involved in a wilderness of dissonance forms, hopelessly confusing to the mind. It would only be possible with greatest difficulty to distinguish between essential and non-essential forms—it being most practical in this connection to define the essential as those in which the idiomatic vitality has been preserved until the climax of the style, and which therefore are most easily recognizable there.[11]

The author hopes to avoid the confusing "wilderness of dissonance forms" and the other difficulties by selecting a dissonance form which has had the "idiomatic vitality" (*Lebensfähigkeit*) to endure not only to the Palestrina period but on down to the present. The pitfalls occasioned by the errors of writing and printing will be avoided, so far as possible, by not basing conclusions on too small a number of examples. The isolated instance may be due to errors in copying, transcribing, or printing, but the likelihood of error diminishes with frequency of occurrence.

The assumption which has here been tacitly made, of the classification of the six-four chord as a dissonance, will find its sufficient justification in the following chapters and therefore need not delay us at this point.

The orientation in the psychological phases of the problem of dissonance treatment has been so thoroughly discussed by Jeppesen that a further statement here does not seem necessary. Likewise with regard to rhythm and accent, Jeppesen's conclusions are assumed to be essentially correct; namely, that, while the accent following the bar line, in the common modern sense can scarcely be considered as holding in the music of the earlier periods under consideration, nevertheless there can be little doubt that there was a well defined feeling for the regular alternation of stress in a two-dimensional rhythm, i.e., the rhythm of the individual voice parts and the resultant rhythm of the whole—a factor which has an interesting parallel in the two-dimensional nature (melodic and harmonic) of the tonal aspects of the music. Morris[12] speaks of ". . . . the

---

[10] *Op. cit.*, pp. 2 ff.      [12] *Contrapuntal Technique in the Sixteenth Century* (London, 1922), p. 37.

[11] *Op. cit.*, p. 3.

accepted metrical rule that the time signature, though without rhythmical significance as regards the individual parts, does yet indicate a regular system of strong and weak harmonic accentuation throughout the composition as a whole."

The modal system is the scalic basis of the music considered in the present work, although by the beginning of the seventeenth century the strict adherence to it was largely broken down and this period marks the transition to the conception of the modern major and minor, as is well known. This change in feeling is most clearly marked in the cadences or cadence formulae. Otherwise the modal influences are present to a considerable extent until a much later period.

It would be an impossible task and also pointless to search out every six-four combination in every composition of every composer in every period. It is possible, however, to go through the works of the more important composers in the various periods in quantity sufficient to set up reliable norms of the procedures in the particular period as a basis for study and classification.

The present study undertakes this research from the beginnings of polyphonic music and carries it through to the middle of the seventeenth century; until the time, namely, when the six-four chord in all its principal forms was fully established in the practice of musical composition, although its common acceptance in the theoretical writings did not occur until approximately a half-century later.[13]

The plan is to illustrate by numerous examples, each one selected from the actual works of the composers and from the most reliable sources available, the gradual evolution of the six-four chord from the varied and more or less incidental occurrences of the earlier periods to the more limited and purposeful use—especially in the cadence formula—of the later periods.

Vienna, 1932                                                            GLEN HAYDON

N. B. In the music the references are to be interpreted as in the following illustration: DTÖ VII, 120,2,2 means *Denkmäler der Tonkunst in Oesterreich*, Vol. VII, p. 120, staff 2, bar 2. If the last figure is preceded by a +, the bars should be counted from right to left; 4,+2, for example, denotes: fourth staff, next to the last bar. For other abbreviations used in connection with works frequently cited, see Bibliography, p. 135.

---

[13] For a concise and yet remarkably comprehensive exposition, with examples, of the use of the six-four chord in later periods, see Bernhard Ziehn, *Manual of Harmony* (Milwaukee, 1907), pp. 71 ff. and the same author's *Harmonie- und Modulationslehre* (Berlin, 1887), pp. 59 ff.

# CHAPTER I

## PRELIMINARIES

THE INTERVAL of the fourth considered as the mathematical relation of 3 to 4 has commonly been accepted as one of the perfect consonances. In musical practice it was early considered highly suitable for use in the combination of melodies, as in the early Organum, where a great many of the compositions consisted of a progression of two voices in parallel fourths. Later, in three or more parts, the preference was given to that position in which the fifth occurred above the lowest voice and the fourth between two upper voices. By the 15th century, the idea seems to have been quite thoroughly established that the fourth, for various, chiefly practical reasons, should be used as a consonant interval only in this relation.

The sixth was quite early accepted as a consonance, although the quality thereof was usually spoken of as imperfect, most probably because it possessed certain qualities of unrest which detracted from its suitability for use in certain situations, as, for example, in relation to the bass in a final chord.

The five-three and six-three combinations have long been considered the "essential" harmonic materials. Other combinations always produced some type of dissonance either between one of the upper parts and the bass, or at least between the two upper parts in places where each upper part when taken separately might be consonant with the bass; for example, the six-five combination. In common practice the term "essential" has been applied to those combinations which were allowed to enter and proceed freely, i.e., without special preparation and resolution; and the term "unessential" to those combinations which have required special treatment with regard to the manner in which they were approached or quitted.

In time, however, with the adoption of a more frankly harmonic point of view, the conception of what constitutes the essential materials has been modified so as to include dissonant combinations and these have gradually come to be used more and more freely. Thus with the increasing familiarity of certain combinations, the unessential of one period has become the essential of the next. This is particularly illustrated in the history of the dominant dissonance of the seventh. The basis for the acceptance of some dissonances and the rejection of others seems to be linked closely with the possibilities of fitting the particular combination into a preconceived scheme of classification of chords as, for example, the idea of all chords being derived from a series of superimposed thirds. From this point of view it may be said that the six-four chord came to be considered as an essential chord because it could be derived from an original position in which notes of the same name stood in the relation of 1, 3, and 5 (root, third, and fifth). The six-five also lent itself to this classification as the second position of a seven-five-three chord. The five-four combination has remained outside the essential chords because it could not be so derived—i.e., it could not be derived from an original combination which stood in the five-three relation or an extension thereof. Such a circumstance as this suggests the possibility of the arbitrary character of our whole system of chord classification. For the five-four combination was doubtless the most frequent and therefore best loved of the early dissonant combinations, and it seems arbitrary, to say the least, to keep it out of the system of essential combinations. It is perhaps receiving

[1]

a belated justification as an essential combination in the hands of modern composers—Debussy was especially fond of it and constantly so used it, i.e., without special preparation and resolution.

On the other hand, the acceptance of the six-four chord as an essential combination has for the most part not saved it from being almost universally treated as unessential (in the earlier sense), i.e., as requiring special treatment of preparation or resolution.

In the periods under consideration the fourth was used in combinations with other intervals such as the seventh, fifth, third, and second. The six-four, four-three, and four-two, under certain restricted treatments, have eventually come to be accepted as essential chords or parts thereof because they could be referred to an original five-three or seven-five-three position, whereas the seven-four has not, because it could not be so referred.[1]

The sixth was used in combination with the seventh (rare), fifth, fourth, third, and second (rare). With the fifth it was often resolved to a six-four on the same bass note, thus bringing this latter chord into greater prominence. The six-three was one of the common essential materials. It was not, however, regarded as consonant enough for the final chord of a composition. Of the remaining combinations the seven-six and six-two were comparatively rare, the latter occurring more often as part of an incomplete chord of the seventh in fourth position or third inversion, i.e., with the chord seventh in the bass. The remaining combination, the six-four, is the subject of the present study, and here the term six-four chord is applied to any simultaneous combination of tones which produce the interval relation of the sixth and fourth as figured above the bass or lowest part. Obviously several factors enter into the problem of determining the relative value or significance of these chords.[2] Of these factors, the relation to the accent, the duration, the movement of the various parts both in approaching and quitting, and, in a certain sense, the degree of the scale on which the combination occurs, would seem to be the most important; and they must all be taken into account in the determination of the full significance of any particular six-four chord.

Before proceeding further with the discussion of the plan of classification, it may be advisable to speak briefly about the use of the word "harmony" in connection with the music of the periods under discussion. The terms *chord, combination,* and *harmony* are used interchangeably as applied to the so-called vertical phenomena. Whether or not the terms as such were in use during any of these particular times need not, at least for the present, enter into the question. Certain it is that consciously or unconsciously what would now commonly be called harmonic considerations did enter into the composition of all the "more-voiced" (*mehrstimmige*) or polyphonic music of the past. This interpretation has recently been strongly advocated by Rudolf Ficker.[3] He says:

It is truly one of the most peculiar and incomprehensible circumstances that up to the present time the whole of musicological research has held doggedly to the fiction that all our European music is to be considered as being derived exclusively from the melodic aspect. . . . . Now our

---

[1] Compare Schönberg, A., *Harmonielehre* (ed. 3; 1922), pp. 478 ff.

[2] The author is aware that some theorists would not honor certain examples with the name "chord" but would simply designate them as passing, unessential, or ornamental phenomena. There may be some justification for this, but there are many reasons why such combinations cannot be passed over so readily. The present author prefers to designate them as chords, in part because it is largely from these very occurrences that the concept of the six-four chord in its indisputable forms has evolved. The frequently repeated and almost axiomatic statement that the unessential of one period often grows into the essential of the next has a direct bearing here.

[3] "Primäre Klangformen," Jahrbuch Peters (1929), p. 21.

polyphony is not, as is so often asserted, a musical phenomenon but a compromise resulting from the balancing of the heterogeneous energetic elements *Klang* (the term *Klang* is here always to be understood in the extended sense of *chord*) and *Melos*. Polyphony arose thus from the fusion (*Verschmelzung*) of two originally quite distinct musical procedures, melodic on the one hand, and harmonic (*klanglichen*) on the other.

Even at the present day this twofold origin of polyphony still continues to exert a lively influence.

In working out a plan for the classification of the six-four chords the author wanted to find as objective a method as possible, and, before the adoption of the actual plan used, he spent a great deal of time trying other systems. In order to make clear something of the difficulties encountered it may be instructive to describe one of the attempts.

In this scheme the movement of the voices in approaching and quitting the six-four chord was made the basis or chief criterion of the classification. The procedure may be described somewhat as follows:

In every six-four combination there must obviously be a minimum of at least three elements, namely,

1. a bass or lowest tone, indicated on the diagram by *B*;
2. a fourth (or its octave above), indicated by the figure *4*; and
3. a sixth (or its octave), indicated on the chart by *6*.

Further, the accompanying types of movement may be classified as:

1. movement by step—indicated on the diagram by *St*;
2. movement by skip—indicated on the diagram by *Sk*;
3. lack of movement, i.e., the part in question being sustained, or stationary, indicated by *Sus*.

Combining these two ideas on the basis that each of the "elements" may be approached by step, by skip, or by sustaining the part from the preceding combination, one gets a total of 27 different possibilities in the approach of the chord, which may be diagrammatically indicated as in the chart on the following page.

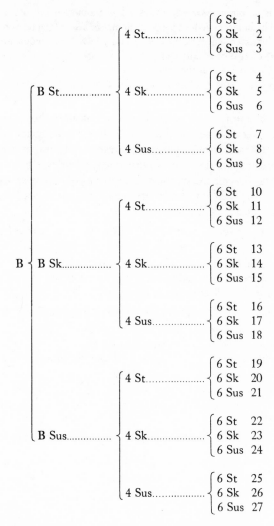

```
                                              ┌ 6 St    1
                            ┌ 4 St............│ 6 Sk    2
                            │                 └ 6 Sus   3
                            │                 ┌ 6 St    4
              ┌ B St.........│ 4 Sk............│ 6 Sk    5
              │             │                 └ 6 Sus   6
              │             │                 ┌ 6 St    7
              │             └ 4 Sus...........│ 6 Sk    8
              │                               └ 6 Sus   9
              │                               ┌ 6 St   10
              │             ┌ 4 St............│ 6 Sk   11
              │             │                 └ 6 Sus  12
              │             │                 ┌ 6 St   13
        B ┤   B Sk..........│ 4 Sk............│ 6 Sk   14
              │             │                 └ 6 Sus  15
              │             │                 ┌ 6 St   16
              │             └ 4 Sus...........│ 6 Sk   17
              │                               └ 6 Sus  18
              │                               ┌ 6 St   19
              │             ┌ 4 St............│ 6 Sk   20
              │             │                 └ 6 Sus  21
              │             │                 ┌ 6 St   22
              └ B Sus.......│ 4 Sk............│ 6 Sk   23
                            │                 └ 6 Sus  24
                            │                 ┌ 6 St   25
                            └ 4 Sus...........│ 6 Sk   26
                                              └ 6 Sus  27
```

Interpreted, this gives the treatment of the individual voices in approaching the six-four chord as follows:

    1. B St, 4 St, 6 St; i.e., the bass is approached by the movement of a step, the fourth likewise, the sixth also;

    2. B St, 4 St, 6 Sk; i.e., bass by step, fourth by step, sixth by skip;

    3. etc.

On the basis of this plan it is possible to classify every six-four chord (the only exception being where one or more of the voices enters after a rest) with respect to the approach, into one of 27 classes. Dividing these further according to the same plan, with respect to the quitting of the chord, one would get 729 types. But while this plan is exhaustive as to the number of possibilities in the approach and quitting of the six-four chord, nevertheless it does not say enough regarding the other factors, especially the relation to the accent, which is very important. The author was compelled, then, to abandon this and similar attempts and to set up a more or less arbitrary plan of classification, which incorporates into a general scheme the more important factors while at the same time it conforms as nearly as possible to the conventional classes in the textbooks.

From the group given above are taken, as essential types, those chords in which, in the approach,

1. the fourth "sustains,"
2. the bass "sustains," and
3. both the fourth and the bass move.

These are then treated with respect to the relation to the accent; the following plan is the result:

I. The accented six-four chord (or relatively or semi- accented). (Nearest relation to the modern cadential six-four chord);

    A. in which the fourth is prepared;

    B. in which the fourth is unprepared.

II. The unaccented six-four chord (or relatively or semi- unaccented);

    A. the auxiliary six-four chord (entering and leaving over a sustained bass);

    B. the passing six-four chord (arising from the use of passing notes or other unessential or decorative notes such as changing-notes, extended auxiliary notes, etc.);

    C. the arpeggio six-four chord[4] (where the fifth of the triad in the bass is approached or quitted by skip while the impression of the continuation of the same chord is maintained by the treatment of the other parts).

This classification affords a working basis suitable for the classification of the majority of six-four chords. A number of comments are necessary. First, with regard to the rhythmic relations and the accent, it has already been stated that the author assumes, in accordance with Jeppesen's procedure, the presence in the periods under discussion of regularly recurring accents which, even in the absence of bar lines, were clearly an ever present factor in the treatment of the dissonance. Thus in the perfect rhythms (3/1 or 3/2) we find a very uniform macro-rhythm (rhythm of the whole) characterized by one relatively stronger accent followed by two less strongly stressed accents. In the imperfect relation (4/1 or 4/2), the first and third were stressed while the second and fourth were unstressed. But it must be further observed that the accent may sometimes be brought about by different means so that while in general the accents may succeed each other in a comparatively uniform manner according to the prevailing rhythmic scheme (i.e., 4/2, 3/2, etc.), these accents may often be shifted by the treatment of the parts. Just what the factors are which bring about these changes from the normal alternating accent may be a debatable point and one which is hard to define, but the movement (or non-movement) of the voices is doubtless one of the important elements. When, for example, there is movement in all the voices to the beginning of a measure, the accentuation is natural; whereas when all the voices sustain in a corresponding place it would generally be conceded that the accent is

---

[4] See p. 7.

either shifted or at least not so strong.[5] Another factor in determining the accent is what happens to the parts after the point in question is passed; and just this difference in treatment may necessitate the shifting of a particular chord from one class to an entirely different one. For example, the following may be classed as an accented

(cadential) six-four chord:  whereas the following:

would be classed as a purely passing phenomenon. It is in order to take care of such chords as these that the terms "relatively" or "semi-accented" and also "relatively" or "semi-unaccented" are used. At the same time it must be remembered that, while the accentuation is a common characteristic of the group I-AB, not all accented six-four chords necessarily belong with this group.

The so-called accented six-four chord (I-AB) includes primarily those six-four chords in which the fourth (usually prepared) is treated as a dissonance resolving down one degree to a third while the bass remains stationary (or skips the octave) and the sixth is free. In modern music this most commonly occurs in the form known as the cadential six-four—occurring with the fifth or first degree[6] of the scale in the bass (in authentic or plagal relation respectively). In the earlier periods it will be seen that this was by no means the usual procedure, and this is the reason why the chord cannot be called the cadential six-four from the beginning. It has been noted, but it will bear repetition, that some of the chords which occur on the accent are, because of the treatment, classed with the group II-B, for example passing combinations (which are usually

unaccented):  or      etc.

In still other instances in which the fourth enters by step on the accent and resolves in the usual manner, it would seem to be a matter of individual feeling or taste whether to leave the chord with the accented six-four chords or to change it to the passing note group.[7] Another item which must be borne in mind in connection with the accented six-four chord is the relation to the cadence formula. This subject will come up for consideration again and again in the succeeding chapters.

The group II-A (unaccented auxiliary six-four chord) has as its chief characteristic, that it occurs over a stationary bass and is usually unaccented. It may occur on what, according to the meter, is the accented portion of the measure, and yet not be an accented six-four chord in the same sense that it would be were the bass approached by movement at this particular point. In such cases the author considers the six-four chord as a type of unaccented or at least semi-unaccented chord.

---

[5] Even this point may be questioned, especially in modern music, if we grant that there is such a thing as a "conceptual" or "mental" accent which may be felt psychologically, if not actually "physically" expressed in the movement or accentuation of the parts themselves.

[6] Throughout the present work the reader should distinguish strictly between the two expressions:

     a) "six-four chord on the second degree of the scale," which for example in C-major would mean:

and   II

     b) 6 , "supertonic six-four chord," which for example in C-major would mean:
        4

[7] See example from Dufay, p. 21 of the present work.

With regard to the class II-B (passing six-four chord) the question of duration plays an increasingly important but not an all important rôle. It may be claimed that this type of six-four chord is of no particular moment,[8] but there can be no question that this type contributed very definitely to the development of the concept of chord inversion.

The "arpeggio" six-four chord II-c in its simplest form is one in which the bass moves arpeggio fashion while the chord is sustained in the upper parts.

Various theorists label this chord differently; for example, Stöhr[9] calls it "Quart-sextakkord mit harmonischer Zerlegung des Basses" and uses the expression "Fehlen des Grundtons im Bass" in further characterizing it. Louis and Thuille[10] speak of it as "Umkehrungsakkord." The author has selected the term "arpeggio" in this connection from the practice of certain English theorists.[11]

There are many variations but they are all characterized by a certain free treatment of the bass, i.e., the approach or quitting of the bass by skip while the harmony does not change. In this form the six-four chord is generally considered to have its clearest significance as the pure inversion of a triad.

The author classes such types as the following under the same heading:

Here the g in the bass is quitted by skip as an "essential" chord note and not as a suspension.

In this case the bass is filled in with passing notes. Remove these and the notes c, e, g, c remain in the bass as essential chord constituents.

It should be borne in mind that these chords come normally under the category of the "unaccented" or "semi-unaccented" chords. On a strong accent they may belong to the accented, prepared six-four chords (class I-A). The determining factor in the classification of such chords is the treatment which follows; for example: if the six-four

---

[8] See Riemann, H., *Musiklexikon* (Berlin, 1929), 2: 1452, on the six-four chord.

[9] Stöhr, R., *Harmonielehre* (ed. 16; Universal ed.; Vienna, 1909), p. 24.    [10] *Op. cit.*, p. 37.

[11] See for example Kitson, C. H., *The Evolution of Harmony* (ed. 2; Oxford Univ. Press, 1924), p. 198.

resolves to a five-three over a stationary bass, it is to be classed as an accented prepared six-four:

whereas the following:

is obviously to be regarded as an arpeggio six-four. The two forms are evidently very closely related.

The author also includes in this category types of free treatment where the skip to or from the bass note comes with a chord change. Here the original meaning has almost if not entirely disappeared but the author deems it the more or less logical outgrowth or extension of the arpeggio idea. In Ockeghem I, 9,4,1,[12] for example, only the skip to the bass remains.

In the earlier periods one is obviously dealing with prototypes of these four forms. Any system of classification is likely to distort the actual significance of some of the chords to which it is applied. In the attempt to simplify, one may occasionally be forced to make a classification which is not entirely satisfactory. In the end, however, the author believes that the system adopted in this work is eminently suited to the exposition of the essential nature of the six-four chord and that its value in this respect compensates many times over for the possible failure to attain, at all times, an absolutely accurate description of the facts.

[12] See p. 39.

# CHAPTER II

## THE THIRTEENTH AND FOURTEENTH CENTURIES

FROM THE EARLIEST TIMES in which three-part compositions are to be found in fairly accurate notation, the six-four chord may be traced. The difficulties of the notation and of its transcription into modern notation are well known. Bellermann,[1] for example, draws attention to the problem and gives the following transcriptions of the same passage from Adam de la Halle (1280), the one by himself, the other by Fétis:

de la Halle
(Bellermann), 35,3,2.

*Ibid.*
(Fétis, Bellermann), 36,1,2.

In this passage the six-four chord appears, although in a different relation, in each transcription. In other situations the six-four chord might disappear, or in still others a slightly different interpretation would bring about new six-four combinations. The tendency of the transcriber to interpret doubtful places in terms of what he thinks is the most sensible harmonic solution by no means assures the researcher that the right solution has been found and that the original intention of the composer is realized. To ascertain these matters in the early periods is especially difficult as Bellermann says,[2] "Harmonisch steht, wie wir sehen, die Kunst noch auf einer sehr niedrigen Stufe. Diese harmonische Mangelhaftigkeit, ja Rohheit, erschwert aber das Notenlesen sehr, da wir nie unser Ohr zu Rathe ziehen können, ob wir bei Uebertragungen das Richtige getroffen haben oder nicht." Pierre Aubry[3] expresses a similar uncertainty: "L'Interprétation des semi-brèves dans les ligatures nous semble encore, bien que dans notre transcription nous ayons dû prendre partie, un problème susceptible de deux solutions," and gives in the following pages an explanation of the two possibilities and his reasons for the one he selects, although he is not entirely satisfied with it nor convinced that it is absolutely the right one. In view of these difficulties one cannot place too much weight on any quotation, but the conclusion may be quite safely drawn that if the changing of any one voice might remove a six-four chord the possibility seems equally good that through this change or changes in other places other six-four chords would put in an appearance. The problem in connection with the 13th and 14th centuries

---

[1] *Mensuralnoten und Taktzeichen des XV. und XVI. Jahrhunderts* (Berlin, 1858), pp. 35 ff. Compare further Wolf, J., *Geschichte der Mensuralnotation von 1250–1460* (Leipzig, 1904), 1:1 ff., and Schering, A., *Geschichte der Musik in Beispielen* (Leipzig, 1931), p. 6.

[2] *Op. cit.*, p. 36.

[3] *Cent Motets du XIIIe Siècle* (Paris, 1908), 3: 51 ff.

then, is to show that the possibilities of the six-four combination occurring were great and that transcriptions of the music actually show a number of these chords. If any particular passage proves to be wrongly interpreted yet the principle remains; not every example can be wrong and there may be many others which only difficulties in the notation prevent from being proved.

In the examples given, many prototypes of later usages occur without the possibility of proving the use of the chord for a definite purpose. They must rather be considered as more or less incidental combinations which might arise in any number of situations from the usual treatment of the parts. Furthermore, many harsher dissonances than those in the six-four combination not only occur but there is also great freedom in their entrance and progression; it hardly seems possible that there should have been any more restraint in the use of the six-four combination than in that of the harsher dissonances.

The example cited by Ludwig,[4] "Alleluja Nativitas," an "Organum triplum" by Perotin, shows a number of examples of the auxiliary six-four combination.

Perotin
(Adler-Ludwig), 226.

Furthermore, the quadruplum, "Viderunt," by Perotin[5] shows a number of similar six-four combinations over a pedal note.

Also in Wolf[6] several such examples are shown:[7]

Petrus de Cruce            *Ibid.*,            *Ibid.*,
(Wolf) III, 3,5,4.         4,3,+1.           5,2,5.

---

[4] Adler-Ludwig, p. 226.

[5] *Ibid.*, pp. 229 ff.

[6] *Op. cit.*, vol. 3.

[7] The accidentals before or above the various notes are given in accordance with those in the source quoted.

Coussemaker's[8] transcriptions from Adam de la Halle show similar examples:

de la Halle
(Coussemaker), 213,3,+2.

*Ibid.,*
268,1,+1.

Compare further 217,1,1; 269,4,+2, etc.

Aubry[9] shows the following examples from the 13th century, which may be regarded as prototypes of the prepared and unprepared six-four used on[10] the second degree, as is found so often in the 15th century.

Aubry II, 59,5,+3.

Aubry II, 227,5,+2.

Examples in abundance of six-four chords of the auxiliary type are also to be found in Aubry's transcriptions,

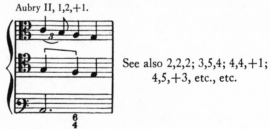

Aubry II, 1,2,+1.

See also 2,2,2; 3,5,4; 4,4,+1; 4,5,+3, etc., etc.

as well as various types of passing six-four chords:

Aubry II, 1,4,+3.

See also 2,3,4; 2,4,3; 139,3,4; etc., etc.

---

[8] *Oeuvres complètes du trouvère Adam de la Halle* (Paris, 1872).    [9] *Op. cit.*    [10] See footnote 6, p. 6.

Further examples of six-four chords of various types in 13th-century music may be found in Wooldridge[11]: 209,1,2; 209,1+1; 209,4,2; 209,4,4/5 etc.[12] 223,3,2; 225,1,3; 225,2,4; etc. (Perotin)[13]; 315,1,1 etc.[14]; and Hughes[15] 39,5,1; 40,4,+1; 53,6,+1, etc.

In the 14th century an examination of the examples given from the *Roman de Fauvel* reveals more six-fours of a similar type, i.e., chiefly six-fours over a stationary bass.

*Roman de Fauvel*[16] (Wolf) III, 9,1,+1.                    *Ibid.*, 9,3,+1.

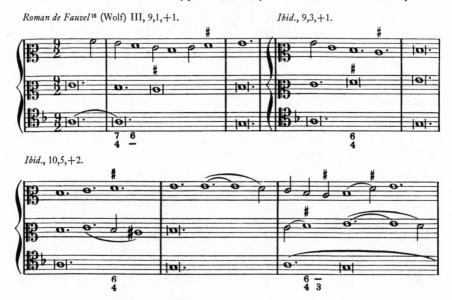

*Ibid.*, 10,5,+2.

Here it appears in a cadence-like formula on the second degree of the scale, a forerunner of a type which became so common in the following century. The following nearly related example may be classed as an accented (or semi-accented) six-four chord in which the fourth is prepared.

*Roman de Fauvel* (Wolf) III, 22,1,+1.

[11] *Oxford History of Music* (Oxford Univ. Press, 1901), vol. 1.

[12] Bibl. Mediceo-Laurenziana, MS Plut. 29. 1, fol. xiv.

[13] *Ibid.*, fol. i.

[14] Mus. Brit. MS, Arundel 248.

[15] *Worcester Mediaeval Harmony of the 13th and 14th Centuries* (Worcester, 1928).

[16] Here and in others of the cited examples from the music of the 13th and 14th centuries the note values are shortened.

For further examples of the auxiliary six-four chord, see *Roman de Fauvel* (Wolf) III, 19,3,1; 19,4,1; 19,4,3; 20,1,2; 20,2,3; 20,2,+1; 20,3,+2; 24,5,+2; 25,1,+2; 26,3,+2; also Machault (Wolf) III, 28,5,+1; 30,4,+1; 32,5,+2; 36,5,1; 37,1,3; 38,3,2; 38,5,2/3; 39,4,1; 40,4,1; 43,1,4; 44,4,3; 46,3,2; 48,3,1; C. Piero (Adler-Ludwig), 284,5,2; F. Landini (Adler-Ludwig), 287,1,+1; 289,4,+2; 290,4,2; and Landini (Ludwig) ZfMW, V, 459,2,+2.

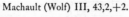

Machault (Wolf) III, 43,2,+2.

The foregoing example might be considered as a sort of 14th-century predecessor of the prepared six-four chord.

The unprepared and free six-four combinations seem to occur more frequently.

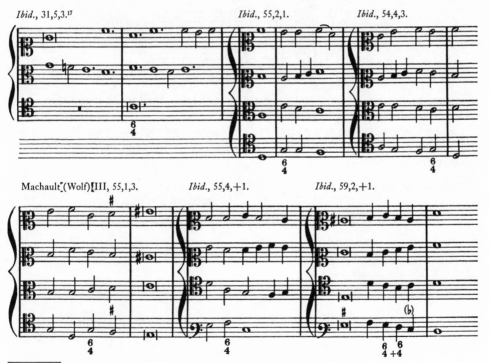

*Ibid.*, 31,5,3.[17]          *Ibid.*, 55,2,1.          *Ibid.*, 54,4,3.

Machault (Wolf) III, 55,1,3.     *Ibid.*, 55,4,+1.          *Ibid.*, 59,2,+1.

[17] See also *ibid.*, 44, 3, 5; Landini (Ludwig), ZfMW 5: 459, 3, +2.

The following are more like passing six-four chords:

Compare further the "Doppelballade" quoted in Adler-Ludwig, 271,2,1; 271,2,2; 272,3,4; 272,3,5.

The following example from Francesco Landini may be classed as a variant of the arpeggio six-four.

Further examples may be found in Wooldridge[18] from an English manuscript dated "late 14th century"—see 106,2,2; 106,3,+2.

From these examples it must be concluded that in the 13th and 14th centuries the occurrence of the six-four chord, although frequent, was primarily an incidental phenomenon.

---

[18] *Op. cit.*, vol. 2.

# CHAPTER III

## THE FIRST NETHERLAND SCHOOL

ROM ITS OCCURRENCE as an incidental phenomenon in the 13th and 14th centuries, the six-four chord advances in the 15th century to a more definite status. It is in that century that material first becomes available in sufficient quantities to make worth while a systematic classification and analysis of its development. The examples are drawn chiefly from the DTÖ (Trienter Codices) and Stainer's *Dufay and His Contemporaries.*

In the music of Dufay which has a close similarity to the "fauxbourdon" style,[1] it is to be expected that six-four chords should occur; as, for example, through delaying the middle part in a succession of parallel six-three chords: etc.

This is obviously the means employed in many of the following examples.

I-A. *The accented (or semi-accented), prepared six-four chord*

The chords of this category fall into two chief classes,

(a) those in which the sixth sustains while the fourth resolves downward by step $\left(\begin{smallmatrix}6-\\43\end{smallmatrix}\right)$;[2]

(b) those in which the sixth moves downward by step along with the fourth $\left(\begin{smallmatrix}65\\43\end{smallmatrix}\right)$.[3]

The fourth is thus treated as a dissonance whereas the sixth is not $\left(\begin{smallmatrix}6-\\43\end{smallmatrix}\right)$.

Dufay DTÖ XIX, 39, 3, +2.[4]        DTÖ XIX, 43, 2, 4.        DTÖ VII, 168, 1, 1.

---

[1] See Adler-Orel, p. 299.

[2] The formula $\begin{smallmatrix}6-\\43\end{smallmatrix}$ was, relatively speaking, seldom used in later periods.

[3] The formula $\begin{smallmatrix}65\\43\end{smallmatrix}$ continued throughout the following centuries, although it was used in different relationships in different periods. In the 15th century, for example, it was chiefly used in the cadence formula but more frequently on the second degree of the scale than on the fifth, as in later periods. Also it should be noticed that the fifth which

follows the sixth in this formula in similar positions a dissonance 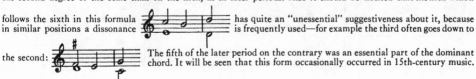 has quite an "unessential" suggestiveness about it, because is frequently used—for example the third often goes down to

the second: The fifth of the later period on the contrary was an essential part of the dominant chord. It will be seen that this form occasionally occurred in 15th-century music.

[4] Unless otherwise indicated the examples are from Dufay.

Compare DTÖ VII, 160, 2,+2; 170,3,+5; 172,2,7; 174,1,5; XIX, 46,3,+2; XXVII, 21,5,4; Dufay (Stainer), 145,2,2; 154,2,+3; 156,2,1; Dunstable DTÖ VII, 189,1,5; 198,2,+2; Dunstable (*E. E. Harm.*) II, 114,3,3; Gilet Velut (Stainer), 194,3,+2; Hubertus de Salinis (about 1420) (Schering), 26,1,4.

In these examples the bass and the sixth enter by step, sometimes in contrary motion (*motus contrarius*), sometimes in similar (*motus rectus*). When in similar motion the relation to the fauxbourdon type of progression becomes apparent. Examples *a* and *b* show cadence-like progressions and it is interesting to note that in each case the six-four is on the second degree of the scale with respect to the final chord in the formula. In other words, the bass moves down by step after the six-four resolves to six-three. Example *b* shows an ornamental treatment of the melody in the upper voice. Other ornamental treatments occur in later examples. It is important to observe these because it will be seen that those which were adapted to a growing sense of harmonic fitness survived into later periods to become essential, integral parts of the technique, while other treatments not so adapted were gradually cast off. This is a notably clear illustration of the evolutionary process, the "survival of the fittest"—fittest in the sense of being most adaptable to new conditions.

In these and the subsequent examples the tendency of the fourth to resolve to the third over a stationary bass should be noticed. This suggests the largely dependent nature of the six-four chord from the beginning.

Similar, except that the sixth as well as the fourth is prepared, are the following:

Dufay DTÖ VII, 123,2,6.          DTÖ VII, 128,3,5.                    DTÖ XI, 80,2,2.

Likewise DTÖ VII, 125,1,+1; 167,2,2; 251,4,4; Cardot (Stainer), 86,3,1.

The sixth often moves to the fifth as the fourth moves to the third. It is characteristic of Dufay (First Netherland School) that this movement usually occurred in the cadence formula on the second degree of the scale with reference to the final.

Dufay DTÖ VII, 160,4,+3.          DTÖ VII, 161,2,2.                    DTÖ VII, 164,4,3.

Similar to *a* are DTÖ VII, 166,3,3; 168,5,2; XI, 78,5,4; XXVII, 30,3,2; to *b*, DTÖ XXVII, 30,4,1. Compare Dufay (Stainer), 108,1,2; 110,2,+1; 116,1,2; Carmen (Stainer), 89,1,2.

Similar but with the fourth and sixth both prepared $\left(\begin{smallmatrix}-65\\-43\end{smallmatrix}\right)$:

Compare Dufay DTÖ VII, 252,1,+3; Dunstable DTÖ VII, 187,3,3; 200,1,7.

The examples *b*, *c*, *d*, and *e* show this type $\left(\begin{smallmatrix}-65\\-43\end{smallmatrix}\right)$ on the fifth degree of the scale with respect to the next chord following the five-three. This is important to note as a prototype of the modern cadential six-four.

Note the characteristic 15th-century treatment in *b* where the bass skips the minor sixth to the third of the succeeding chord, also in *d*, where the skip is that of the octave, and in *e* where the skip is a major sixth. Such examples, particularly *b*, deal a severe blow to the theory that the music of the 15th century is merely an association of melodies and the harmonies are incidental by-products. Surely such a part would not be written for the "beauty of the melodic line" (in the construction of which wide skips were generally avoided, and particularly two in the same direction). No, this and similar examples show quite positively that the harmonic attitude was strongly developed. Examples *f* and *g* show this $\frac{65}{43}$ used in the course of a phrase with no particular cadential effect.

The following examples show typical ornamental variations of the resolution of the $^{65}_{43}$ on the second degree of the scale with respect to the final.

Compare Cesaris (Stainer), 97,1,+3; DTÖ VII, 178,2,5.

Example *d* occurs again in Dufay (Stainer), 154,2,+3.

See further Carmen (Stainer), 92,2,2; Dufay (Stainer), 137,2,+3.

The fact that six-fours of this type (i.e., with the fourth prepared and resolved downward one degree) also occurred on other degrees of the scale than the second and fifth shows that the dominant feeling was as yet by no means fully developed.[5] The

---

[5] It is interesting to note that when the six-four comes on the fifth degree of the scale it is commonly thought of as having primarily a dominant character, i.e., it is a decoration of the dominant chord to which it resolves or the appearance of which it delays. When the six-four comes on the second degree of the scale it is still commonly thought of as a dominant chord or as having a dominant character, the fourth commonly resolving to the third of a $\overset{VII}{6}$ which is held to be a $\overset{V}{7}$ with root omitted. That the sixth should go to the fifth and then skip up a third to the final may be considered as a decorative process. It also suggests the presence of a considerable amount of dominant feeling in the II itself under certain conditions.

following examples show the six-four chord on other degrees, sometimes quite near the cadence formula if not an actual part of it.

Compare Dufay DTÖ XI, 80,2,2 (see p. 16) and XXVII, 30,3,+4.

It should be noted that in *a* and *c* the bass skips as the fourth resolves, in connection with which, however, in *a* the note of resolution is anticipated. Such resolutions, i.e., those with a skip in the bass, are rare in 15th-century technique. Compare further:

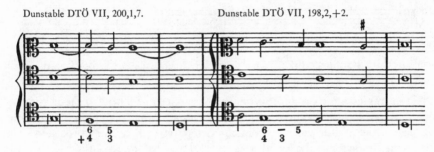

I-B. *The accented (or semi-accented), unprepared six-four chord*

In the following examples the unprepared, accented six-four chord has been used on the fifth or first degree of the scale in a cadence formula.

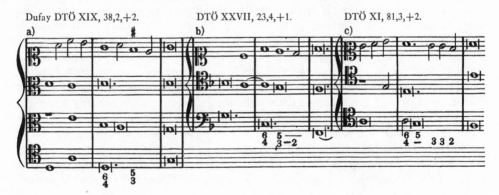

G. Velut (Stainer), 195,1,2.

Dufay (Stainer), 139,2,3.

Dufay (Stainer), 150,2,+1.

Dunstable DTÖ VII, 186,5,+4.

Dufay (Stainer), 139,1,3.

Compare Dufay (Stainer), 105,2,2 (in a deceptive cadence); 106,1,2; also Cesaris (Stainer), 97,2,+1; 98,1,2.

These examples are clear prototypes of the modern cadential six-four chord. The example *h* is like a deceptive cadence. The melodic idiom of the upper voice of *a, b, c,* and the octave skip in the middle voice of *c* are characteristic 15th-century procedures.[6] That the dissonant character of the fourth was felt is shown by the resolution to the third in each case, whereby, however, ornamental resolutions such as *a* were not excluded.

From an evolutionary standpoint this treatment of the six-four chord in the fifteenth century must be considered more or less accidental. Such treatment, because of certain characteristics with respect to the tonal feeling, could only gradually, in the course of generations, come to be consciously used to produce a particular effect. The freer treatment of the fourth is to be expected in a period in which all dissonances were used more freely. Gradually, as is well known, there was a refinement in the use of dissonance up to the time of Palestrina[7] and this is true, as will be seen, of the use of the six-four. Even the presence of a relatively large number of these accented unprepared six-four chords in the music of Dufay and his contemporaries is scarcely sufficient ground for reaching the conclusion that the six-four chord in its modern sense was consciously used by the composers of that period, as is suggested by Stainer[8] when he says: "The second inversion of the common chord has generally been considered of modern growth, but it is of frequent occurrence, sometimes preceded by preparation, as if discordant, at others, without preparation." That the six-four chord was common at that time, is obvious, but to assume that it was considered the second inversion of the common chord is hardly justifiable.

[6] Compare Adler-Orel, p. 306.
[7] Compare Jeppesen, *op. cit.*, pp. 264 ff.
[8] *Dufay and His Contemporaries* (London, 1898), p. 38.

In the following examples, although the fourth is unprepared, its use is suggestive of an accented passing note.

Dufay DTÖ VII, 145,1,4.  DTÖ XXVII, 29,6,+2.          DTÖ XXVII, 30,3,2.

Example *c* is an interesting variation of *b*—the general similarity of the melodic lines is obvious; only slight rhythmical alterations produce different chordal combinations.

Dufay (Stainer), 147,1,2.                    Dufay (Stainer), 107,1,+3.

In *d* the six-four occurs on the sixth degree of the scale with respect to the cadence which immediately follows. This procedure, which occurs rarely in the 15th century, foreshadows a device which was common in the 16th. In Dufay, it is like an accented passing combination, whereas in Palestrina it is commonly introduced as a suspension.[9] Example *e* is interesting as showing an unusual relation of the six-four to the cadence formula, i.e., on the third degree.

Compare DTÖ VII, 146,4,5; 162,3,2; XI, 80,2,1; Hubertus de Salinas (Schering), 26,1,4; 26,2,4.

Sometimes the six-four chord resulted when the fourth came in as a sort of auxiliary or returning note.

Dufay DTÖ XIX, 38,2,4.    DTÖ VII, 182,3,5.    DTÖ VII, 155,2,1.    Dunstable DTÖ VII, 199,3,+3.

Compare DTÖ VII, 169,3,5; 173,1,+4; Acourt (Stainer), 51,1,1; Dufay (Stainer), 122,1,+1; Cesaris (Stainer), 97,3,+1.

[9] Compare pp. 16 and 64 f.

And occasionally when the fourth is approached by skip in an appoggiatura-like procedure:

Compare Dufay (Stainer), 128,2,+1, in which the harmonic effect is: $\begin{smallmatrix}\text{I V I}\\6\\4\end{smallmatrix}$ but in 15th-century trimmings $\left(\begin{smallmatrix}6\text{-}5\text{-}\\4332\end{smallmatrix}\right)$. And only rarely quite free:

Compare Dunstable DTÖ VII, 195,4,+2 (accented six-four with fourth quitting by skip of third up).

## II-A. *The auxiliary six-four chord*

Usually the fourth enters and progresses by step either as an ascending or descending passing note or as an auxiliary or returning note. It may also be held over as a continuation of a previous suspension $\left(\begin{smallmatrix}\smile 765\\ \smile 4\text{-}3\end{smallmatrix},\ \text{etc.}\right)$. Less frequently is it approached or quitted by skip. The sixth seems to be quite free—the strongest six-four feeling probably arising when it progresses in similar motion with the fourth, provided, of course, the chord is prominent in other respects—i.e., accented or semi-accented and of relatively long duration.

1. Fourth as an ascending passing note:

---

[10] The printed edition has *c* here (*) but the note indicates a *g* in the original.

Compare DTÖ XIX, 33,2,+3; Dunstable DTÖ VII, 188,3,+1; 190,3,5; 202,5,+3; 206,3,3; *E. E. Harm.* II, 116,3,5.

2. Fourth as a descending passing note:

Dufay DTÖ XIX, 24,4,+2.        Binchois (Stainer), 72,3,+2.

Compare DTÖ XIX, 27,3,5; 36,3,+1; XXVII, 23,4,1; VII, 164,4,3; 169,3,5; 171,2,+2; 173,1,+4; Dufay (Stainer), 143,2,1; 143,2,+1; R. Libert (Stainer) 177,3,+3; Lionel Power (Schering), 131,7,3.

3. Fourth as an auxiliary note:

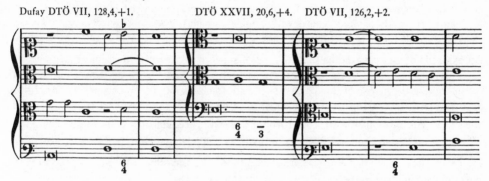

Dufay DTÖ VII, 128,4,+1.        DTÖ XXVII, 20,6,+4.    DTÖ VII, 126,2,+2.

Compare Dunstable VII, 206,3,+1; Dufay (Stainer), 124,3,3. Binchois (Stainer), 72,3,+2; also Cesaris (Stainer), 96,1,1.

The following is a further example of an auxiliary six-four in a more obviously modern relation although with the characteristic octave skip of the contratenor.[11]

Binchois (Stainer), 64,1,2.

---

[11] Compare Jeppesen, *op. cit.*, p. 213 and p. 68 of the present work.

4. Fourth approached or quitted by skip:

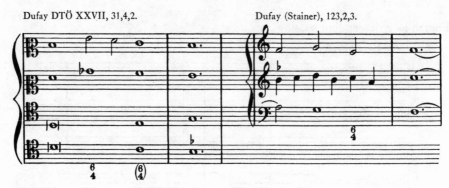

Dufay DTÖ XXVII, 31,4,2.          Dufay (Stainer), 123,2,3.

Compare Dufay (Stainer), 144,1,3.

5. Fourth held over from previous suspension:

The double suspension of the seventh and fourth was one of the favorite devices of the 15th century. Jeppesen[12] says:

About 1450 it was greatly preferred to all other syncopations. In the course of a century, however, it had fallen into disuse, and in Palestrina we find it only employed as an exception.

Instead of it, the six-four chord with double ties played a prominent rôle with Italian composers, while the Netherlanders seem not to have appreciated the tonal beauty of this effect.

An example of an accented cadential type of six-four is given from Palestrina.

The author of the present work would point out another line of development in connection with the use of this particular double suspension, in which the six-four chord occurred with increasing frequency until it came to be a regular constituent of one of the most common forms of the 16th and early 17th centuries—namely, the $\left\{ \begin{smallmatrix} 65- \\ 4-3 \end{smallmatrix} \right.$ combination.[13] The process of evolution may be traced somewhat as follows:

First, the $\overset{76}{\underset{43}{\smile}}$ suspension was most common, the movement of the upper parts in parallel fourths being apparently not at all objectionable.

Dunstable DTÖ VII, 198,1,5.

Parallel fourths occasionally occur even between the two lower parts.

---

[12] *Op. cit.*, p. 231.

[13] The sign $\{$ indicates that different combinations may precede the six-four chord.

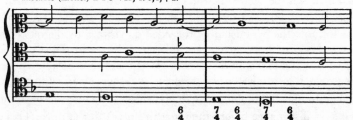

Dunstable (Lionel) DTÖ VII, 196,4,+2.

Nevertheless, these parallel fourths were frequently avoided by first bringing the seventh to the sixth and then resolving the fourth on the next beat. Thus a relatively unaccented (semi-unaccented) six-four chord arose.

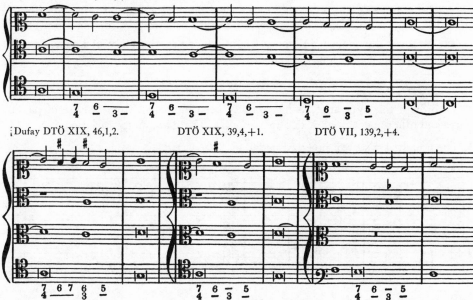

Dunstable DTÖ VII, 199,2,4 ff.

¦Dufay DTÖ XIX, 46,1,2.          DTÖ XIX, 39,4,+1.          DTÖ VII, 139,2,+4.

Compare Dunstable DTÖ VII, 192,4,4; 192,5,7; 193,3,2; 197,4,2; Dufay (Stainer), 121,2,3; Cesaris (Stainer), 98,1,+2; Randulfus Romanus (Stainer), 184,1,+2; etc.

The $\overset{\frown}{7}_5$ and $\overset{8}{\underset{4}{}}$ and other combinations at times occurred instead of the $\overset{\frown}{7}_4$ of this formula.

Dunstable DTÖ VII, 200,1,+2.          Dunstable DTÖ VII, 197,4,+4.

Compare Dunstable DTÖ VII, 202,2,5, etc.

At this point it will be seen that the common relation is $\frac{76\text{--}5}{4\text{--}3\text{--}}$ in which the fourth resolves to the third before the sixth goes to the fifth. It should also be noticed that following this formula the bass usually proceeded downward by degree to the final, or, in other words, the formula occurred on the second degree of the scale. Later, as the feeling for dissonant treatment became more refined and as the value of the use of the dissonance in producing strong rhythmical effects was more clearly appreciated, another variation came into more common use, namely, the $\left\{ \frac{65\text{--}}{4\text{--}3} \right.$.[14] Here the sixth moves to the fifth, forming a $\underset{4}{5}$ dissonance before the fourth resolves to the third. This came to be used chiefly on the fifth[15] or the first degree of the scale.

These two lines of development of the six-four chord are both important because they show the twofold nature of the chord. *Accented*, it is essentially discordant, having preparation and resolution. *Unaccented*, it has largely consonant characteristics in that the fourth may serve in the formula under consideration not only as the resolution of the $\underset{5}{6}$ dissonance but also as the preparation of the following $\underset{4}{5}$ combination. The $\underset{4}{5}$ as the stronger dissonance was more frequently given the place of honor, i.e., the position of greatest stress, in the cadence formula.

### II-B. *The passing six-four chord*

Chords of this type arise, as has already been indicated, from the use of passing notes and other unessential or decorative notes. There are many variations:

1. The fourth as a sort of inverted pedal:

Dufay DTÖ VII, 155,3,2.  DTÖ VII, 149,5,+1.      DTÖ VII, 154,2,+4.      DTÖ VII, 158,2,3.

2. Passing note combinations in the bass:

Dufay DTÖ VII, 132,3,3.     DTÖ VII, 137,3,5.     DTÖ XI, 78,4,+1.     DTÖ VII, 152,3,+2.

---

[14] See for example p. 35, etc.

[15] In this situation the passing seventh was often added to the five-three on the dominant, which of course was an important step in the evolution of the dominant seventh chord.

Compare DTÖ VII, 166,4,+2; Binchois (Stainer), 75,3,+1; Guillermus Malbecque (Stainer), 180,1,+1; Gilet Velut (Stainer), 194,2,+1.

3. Passing notes in upper parts:

Dufay DTÖ XIX, 30,3,+2.    DTÖ XXVII, 20,1,+3.    DTÖ VII, 252,3,+1.           DTÖ VII, 132,4,3.

Dufay (Stainer), 124,2,+1.

Compare  DTÖ VII, 178,3,2;  XIX, 44,3,5;  XXVII, 19,4,+1;  30,3,1; Dunstable DTÖ VII, 189,5,3; 190,2,+1; 196,5,+2; 206,3,3; Gilet Velut (Stainer), 194,3,1.

4. Use of extended auxiliary or changing notes:

Dufay DTÖ VII, 136,2,5.  DTÖ VII, 162,2,+2.           DTÖ VII, 183,2,1.          DTÖ XXVII, 30,1,+2.

Compare Dufay (Stainer), 127,2,1.

See also DTÖ VII, 144,3,+5; 160,2,+3; 160,4,+1; 165,4,3; 168,2,+2; XI,77,2,3; 78,5,3; 79,2,3; 79,5,+2; 81,1,+2; XXVII, 30,2,+1; 31,2,+4; Dufay (Stainer), 104,1,+1; Binchois (Stainer), 80,2,5.

5. The use of the anticipation could also produce a six-four combination:

Another type of six-four which occurs in the works of Dufay a number of times is difficult to explain other than as some sort of syncopation of a passing note, or should it be said that the six-four sometimes resolved through the bass's *moving a step up?*

Dufay DTÖ VII, 150,2,7.     DTÖ VII, 161,3,3.     DTÖ VII, 161,4,+4.     DTÖ VII, 163,3,2.

Dufay DTÖ VII, 166,1,1.                     DTÖ VII, 162,1,2.

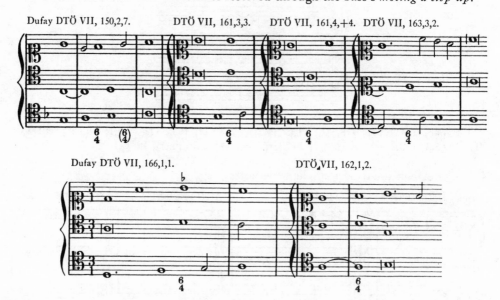

In the last example the fourth is quitted by skip as the bass moves up by degree.

Compare Dufay (Stainer), 114,2,+3; 117,2,3; 146,1,2; Dunstable DTÖ VII, 200,2,7.

## II-c. *The arpeggio six-four chord*

In the following examples the free entrance of the bass note is perhaps the strongest direct evidence of the presence in the 15th century of a feeling for the six-four combination as an independent chord.

Dufay DTÖ XIX, 34,1,+1.     DTÖ XXVII, 32,5,5.     DTÖ VII, 168,4,+2.

Dufay (Stainer), 127,2,+2.     Dufay (Stainer), 128,1,3.

The harmonic effect of the example Dufay (Stainer), 127,2,2, is clearly $\begin{smallmatrix} I & V \\ 6 & 5 \\ 4 & 3 \end{smallmatrix} \Big| \begin{smallmatrix} I \\ 5 \\ 3 \end{smallmatrix}$. The skip to and from the fourth gives prominence to the six-four combination as an "essential" chord.

These examples should be compared with: DTÖ XXVII, 19,4,1; DTÖ XIX, 38,2,5; DTÖ VII, 182,3,5; Acourt (Stainer), 51,1,1; Dufay (Stainer), 118,2,3; Dunstable DTÖ VII, 206,1,+6; 206,3,+3; *E. E. Harm.*, 117,2,1.

The following example does not lend itself to classification in any of the above categories. It has, however, a certain suggestive relation to a cadence formula.

Carmen (Stainer), 91,2,+1.

The examples cited in this chapter show the frequent occurrence of the six-four chord in the compositions of the 15th century. The period is an important one not only in the evolution of the six-four chord but also in the history of music as a whole because here the fundamental principles in the treatment of the dissonance, which have dominated the technique of musical composition throughout the succeeding centuries, were beginning to find expression in the works of composers and theorists. Thirds and sixths became more clearly established in theory and practice as consonances and fourths as dissonances, even if mild ones.[16] The concept of the passing or ornamental dissonance and of the syncope was growing more definite and the uses thereof were more clearly stated.

---

[16] See pp. 128 ff.

# CHAPTER IV

## THE SECOND NETHERLAND SCHOOL

THE LEADER of the Second Netherland School was Ockeghem, and in his works are continued the principal types of the six-four chord as found in Dufay and his contemporaries.

I-A. *The accented (or semi-accented), prepared six-four chord*

The following examples show the $\underset{\smile 43}{6-}$ formula:

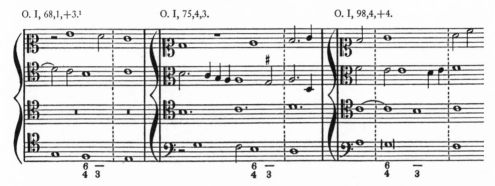

Compare Ockeghem I, 54,1,5; and Jeppesen[2]: 32,3,2; 43,5,+2; 55,4,5; 57,5,1; 62,2,2 (Ockeghem); 63,5,2 (Ockeghem).

Various more or less ornamental resolutions of the fourth occur, in most of which the duration of the dissonance is shortened:

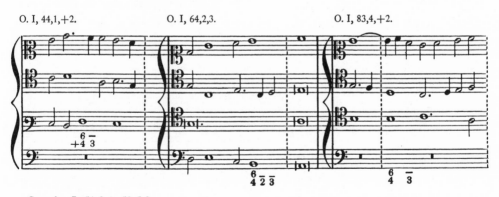

See also I, 51,2,4; 59,5,3.

---

[1] See Bibliography, under Ockeghem.

[2] *Der Kopenhagener Chansonnier* (Leipzig and Kopenhagen, 1927). According to Jeppesen (p. XXXVII), the musical context appears to belong exclusively to the Busnois-Ockeghem generation.

In certain other examples the fourth apparently resolves on a note of short duration such as a quarter note:

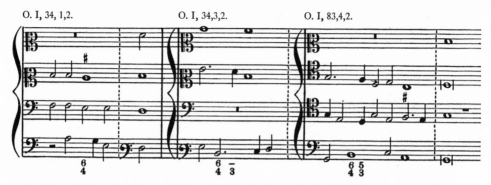

Compare Jeppesen, 1,5,1; 15,5,3 (P. Baziron); 53,4,2 (Ockeghem); 60,2,3 (Busnois).

In the following example the fourth moves to the third (a quarter note) but it is also possible to consider the *e* in the lowest part as an ascending passing note and the *g* of the upper voice an ornamental note:

The following variations in the treatment of the six-four should be noted in connection with the $_{43}^{6-}$ group:

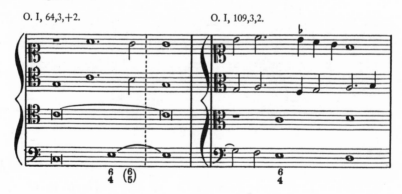

In the next example, O. I, 53,5,+1 ("Missa cujusvis toni"), Kade[3] states that the second note in the upper voice should apparently be a degree lower, giving: $\underbrace{5\text{----}}_{4323\text{-}}$

O. I, 53,5,+1.

No reason is given but the implication is that Kade thought the five-four was more frequent in this relation in Ockeghem's work; or it may be he was influenced by the fact that this resolution occurs so commonly in the later periods. Be that as it may, the $\underbrace{6\text{-}}_{43}$ combination is so usual with Ockeghem, as the preceding examples show, that it is obviously entirely in accordance with his style to find it here.

The following examples will illustrate Ockeghem's use of the $\underbrace{65}_{43}$ formula.

O. I, 100,5,2.          O. I, 104,2,+2.          O. I, 51,5,4.

Compare O. I, 114,3,+2; and Jeppesen, 55,4,5; 57,5,1; 62,2,+1 (Ockeghem); 63,4,+1 (Ockeghem); 63,5,+2 (Ockeghem).

O. I, 6,1,3.          O. I, 51,2,5.          O. I, 111,1,+2.

---

[3] Ambros, A. W., *Geschichte der Musik* (ed. 2; Leipzig, 1880–1882), "Beispielband," vol. 5:5,2,3.

Compare O. I, 104,2,+1 (cited on page 40 of the present work) and Jeppesen 63,5,+2.

In the following example the fourth moves up in parallel fourths with the next lower voice, which then takes the note of resolution.

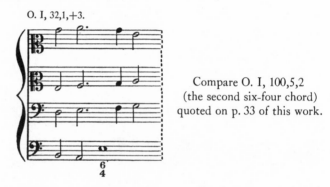

Compare O. I, 100,5,2
(the second six-four chord)
quoted on p. 33 of this work.

### I-B. *The accented (or semi-accented), unprepared six-four chord*

This type of the six-four chord occurs in Ockeghem but the fourth is usually approached and quitted in conjunct motion, so that it may be analyzed as an accented auxiliary or passing note. The first example below is an exception in that the fourth enters after a rest and moves in an unusual manner ornamentally upward a degree to a consonance.

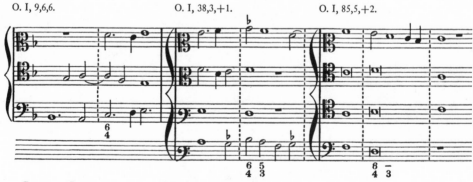

Compare Jeppesen, 4,1,+1 (Morton); 4,5,2 (Morton); 9,1,2; 39,5,2.

In the following examples the skips in the bass make the six-four chord more prominent:

O. I, 40,3,+3.

II-A. *The auxiliary six-four chord*

The six-four chord occurs frequently with the fourth treated as an ascending passing note.

O. I, 61,1,+4.

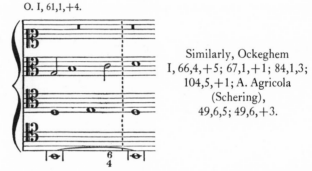

Similarly, Ockeghem
I, 66,4,+5; 67,1,+1; 84,1,3;
104,5,+1; A. Agricola
(Schering),
49,6,5; 49,6,+3.

Ockeghem I, 113,4,+3 shows it with the fourth as a type of descending passing note in the $\left\{ \begin{smallmatrix} 65- \\ 4-3 \end{smallmatrix} \right.$ formula which has already been mentioned. See p. 26 of this work.

O. I, 113,4,+2.

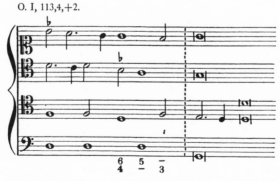

See A. Agricola (Schering), 49,2,+4; 49,6,+2; and Jeppesen 35,5,+2 (Prioris).

An interesting example in which the fourth is used as an auxiliary note occurs:

O. I, 1,2,1.

The following variations[4] are from the same composition, "Missa sine nomine."

O. I, 15,1,4.                          O. I, 27,4,+2.

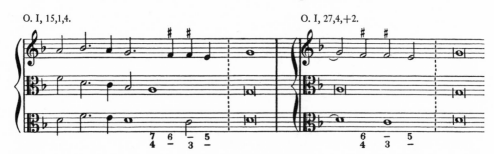

Compare O. I, 15,3,2; 16,2,+1; 17,1,+2; 21,3,2; 21,6,+2; and Jeppesen 15,1,+2 (P. Baz-iron); 17,2,3 (Busnois); 21,1,+3; 22,3,2; 23,4,+2; 30,1,+1; 30,4,3; 31,4,+3; 42,2,+2; 63,1,1 (Ockeghem).

## II-B. *The passing six-four chord*

1. The fourth like an inverted pedal or short organ point with the bass moving as a passing or auxiliary note:

O. I, 24,1,+2.              O. I, 104,3,1.

Compare O. I, 61,2,5; 63,1,1; and Jeppesen, 5,4,+3 (Convert?); 6,1,+1 (Convert); 30,3,+1 (2 examples); 46,3,+3; 58,4,+2 (Magister Symon); 63,5,1 (Ockeghem).

---

[4] Compare with p. 24.

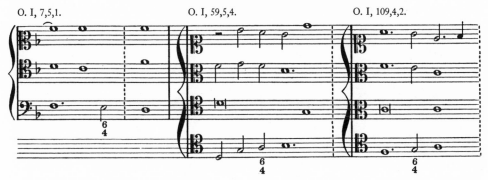

Compare O. I, 49,5,+4; 64,4,3; 71,1,+2; 74,7,3; 79,3,1; and Jeppesen, 7,4,4 (Hayne); 14,3,2 (P. Baziron); 29,5,2.

With more than four-part writing this type occurs less frequently.

2. Passing notes in the upper parts:

Compare Jeppesen, 15,1,4 (P. Baziron); 16,3,2 (Busnois); 19,3,3 (Busnois); 21,3,3; 37,3,2 (Morton); 40,4,+1; 54,2,+2.

That such combinations were not without chordal feeling, i.e., that they were not merely passing or ornamental occurrences is shown by such an example as the following,

in which the skip of the fourth up to *g* from the *d* suggests that it was thought of simply as a skip from one tone to another of the same chord. If this is true then the feeling of chord inversion may have been present long before the theorists gave formal utterance to the idea.[5]

---

[5] See Riemann, H., *Geschichte der Musiktheorie* (Leipzig, 1898), pp. 372 and 431.

3. Six-four chords resulting

(*a*) from a combination in which the fourth is treated as a sort of extended auxiliary in an upper part:

Compare Jeppesen, 27,1,3; 33,4,+3; 50,4,3.

(*b*) from the use of a variation of a changing note device in the bass or upper parts:

See O. I, 66,3,+3; 72,5,6; 109,4,2; and Jeppesen, 23,2,+2.

(*c*) from the use of an anticipation:

Compare Jeppesen, 47,5,3; 59,2,4 (Magister Symon).

The situation in which the bass moves up by step from a six-four chord while the other notes sustain occurs relatively more frequently in Ockeghem than in Dufay.[6]

---
[6] See p. 28.

See O. I, 14,6,3; 50,5,3; 60,5,4; 76,5,+2; 77,2,1; 85,1,+1; 93,4,3; and Jeppesen 63,3,+2 (Ockeghem).

### II-c. *The arpeggio six-four chord*

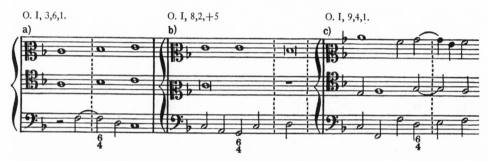

To *a*, compare O. I, 3,6,6; 95,4,+3; and Jeppesen, 63,1,2 (Ockeghem).

To *b*, compare O. I, 104,1,+1 and I, 57,3,2.

Example *c* might also be classed as a variation of the so-called passing six-four arising from the use of unaccented (or semi-unaccented) auxiliary or decorative notes. See p. 8; and compare also Ziehn, *Man. of Harm.*, p. 73.

In *e*, O. I, 34,3,2, the skip to the *d* in the bass while the other parts sustain, together with the fact that the *f* in the middle part is shorter than the usual note of resolution of a suspension and has rather a changing note character, lends strength to the idea of the six-four chord as a variation of the arpeggio type.

To *f*, compare O. I, 112,5,4.

---

[7] This measure lacks a half note of being complete in the bass.

O. I, 100,5,2.                       O. I, 104,2,+1.

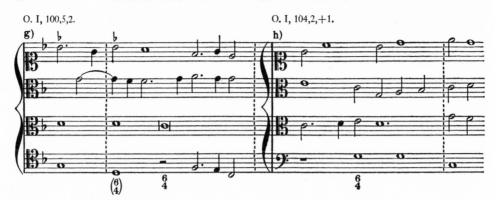

In the following examples, in one way or another, the six-four chord is brought into a certain prominence.

O. I, 65,1,3.            O. I, 85,2,2.            O. I, 14,5,2.

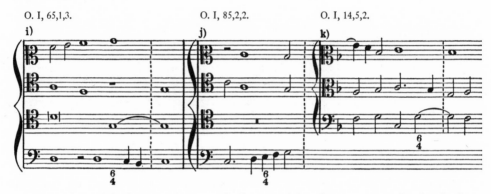

Example *i* might be regarded as a six-four resulting from a suspension in the bass with an ornamental resolution. The author prefers to class it with the arpeggio six-fours as a variation of *a* (p. 39).

Examples *h* and *j* can also be classed as variations of the accented prepared six-four.[8]

Example *k* stands in an intermediate position between the accented, prepared six-four and the arpeggio. Attention has already been directed to the close relation between certain of these forms.[9]

So far as the six-four chord is concerned, there seems to be but little change in the Second Netherland School from the procedures of Dufay and his contemporaries. All the older types continue to appear, but on the whole the dissonance is treated with more care. For example, the accented unprepared six-four is relatively less common. In the period that follows, however, a more decided change of attitude toward the use of the six-four chord becomes manifest.

---

[8] See p. 7 f., and compare Jeppesen, 4,5,1.

[9] See p. 7 f.

# CHAPTER V

## THE THIRD NETHERLAND SCHOOL

JOSQUIN DES PRÈS, leader of the Third Netherland School, perpetuated in his works many of the characteristics of the earlier schools with respect to the use of the six-four chord, but at the same time the proportion of types which more closely resemble the modern[1] uses, greatly increases. The critical issue seems to be in relation to the cadence formula. Here the point of view seems to undergo several remarkable changes but it is, as might be expected, still far removed from the purely modern conception, as such an example as the following clearly shows.

Jos. W. I, 11,2,+1.[2]

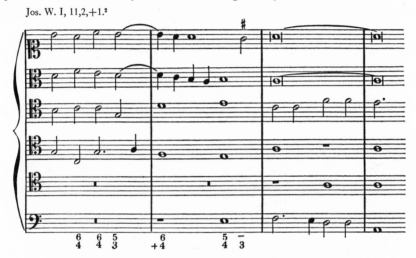

I-A. *The accented (or semi-accented), prepared six-four chord*

The $\frac{6-}{43}$ combination continues to appear but relatively less frequently. It occurs on the second degree of the scale in a cadence formula:

Jos. M. I, 4,4,2.          Jos. M. I, 130,2,5.

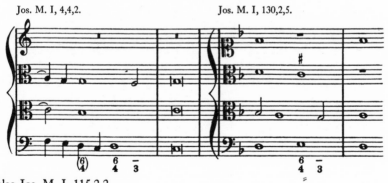

See also Jos. M. I, 115,2,2.

---

[1] When not otherwise expressly indicated, the author uses the term "modern" to indicate quite generally that music which is based upon the major and minor scales instead of the ecclesiastical modes.

[2] See Bibliography, under Josquin des Près.

It also occurs on the sixth degree of the scale just before or as a part of a cadence formula:

Compare other examples of the $\frac{6-}{43}$ formula: Jos. M. I, 71,5,+1; 102,2,+2 (three examples in two measures, the suspended fourth resolving on the second quarter); W. I, 11,2,+1 (cited on p. 41); 38,2,+3 (not actually a six-four but worth studying in connection with the foregoing examples).

In the majority of occurrences, however, the sixth moves to the fifth as the fourth resolves to the third ($\begin{smallmatrix} 65 \\ 43 \end{smallmatrix}$). There is a growing tendency to use this accented six-four chord in a cadence-like progression, i.e., where the bass skips a fourth up or a fifth down from the five-three chord:

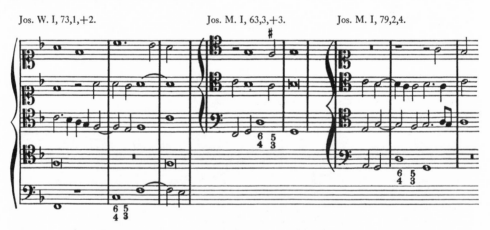

Or where a similar effect is produced by the entrance of another voice, or by the device, which earlier was used much more frequently, in which the tenor crosses the lower part and then skips the octave:

Jos. M. I, 8,3,3.                          Jos. M. I, 106,4,+2.

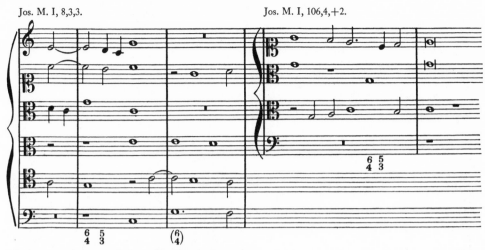

Or in a more extended cadencing progression:

Jos. W. I, 84,1,+1.                        Jos. W. I, 71,2,4.

Compare de Orto (Amb. V), 200,2,3; Layolle (Amb. V), 203,2,3; 203,3,3; H. Isaac (Amb. V), 329,3,1.

Josquin also uses this type of accented six-four chord on the second degree but more often on the sixth degree—so that at times the six-four chord on the sixth degree is followed in the next measure by one on the fifth degree in a cadence formula:

Jos. M. I, 95,2,+3.                        Jos. M. I, 32,5,+3.[3]

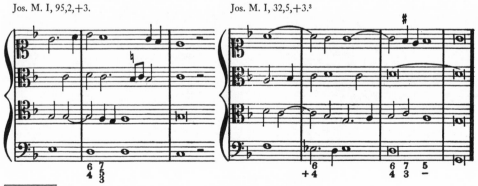

_____

· [3] In the latter example the interesting use of the seventh should be noted.

Compare Jos. W. I, 11,2,+1 (cited on p. 41); 38,2,+2; Genet (Amb. V), 224,3,1; Isaac (Amb. V), 349,2,3; Ghiselin (Amb. V), 192,2,1.

In addition to the above-mentioned uses, the accented $\underset{43}{65}$ is also used in the course of a phrase outside the cadence formula or with a deceptive cadence effect:

Jos. W. I, 22,2,4.                                     Jos. M. I, 6,2,+2.

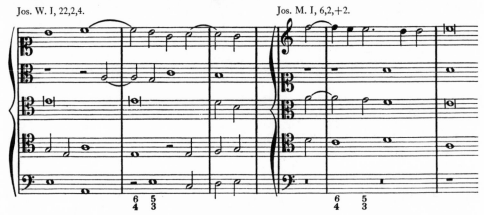

Compare further Jos. W. I, 40,3,+1; Jos. M. I, 56,1,+3; 71,5,+3; 79,5,4; 79,5,+1; 82,2,3; Brumel (Amb. V), 153,2,+1; H. Fink (Amb. V), 247,4,2; 266,4,1 (with octave skip in bass); Stolzer (Riemann, *Hdb. d. MG.*) II,178,2,2; Layolle (Amb.V), 206,2,1; Genet (Amb.V), 220,2,1.

### I-B. *The accented (or semi-accented), unprepared six-four chord*

This type seems to have practically disappeared except in such an example as Jos. W. I, 11,2, +2,[4] in which the fourth is prepared in one voice and skipped to in another. Compare Isaac (Amb. V), 354,2,+1; Stolzer (Riemann, *op. cit.,*) II, 180,2,1.

### II-A. *The auxiliary six-four chord*

The favorite combination now seems to be $\left\{ \begin{matrix} 65- \\ 4-3 \end{matrix} \right.$ after which the bass often skips a fourth up or a fifth down in a cadence-like progression. The beginnings of this formula have been pointed out[5] in the chapter on the First Netherland School, where the six-four chord often follows a double suspension of the seventh and fourth $\underset{4}{\overset{7}{\smile}}$.

In the following example the six-five comes on the accent and resolves on the six-four.

Jos. M. I, 82,4,4.

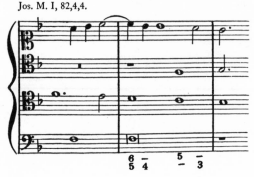

---

[4] Cited p. 41.     [5] Pp. 23 ff.

Here, as has already been said, the six-four chord plays a somewhat more important rôle because the fourth serves not only as the resolution of the six-five dissonance but also as a preparation of the dissonance in the succeeding five-four combination. The strong rhythmical resultant effect of the progression seemed to make it very desirable for the cadence formula and it continued to find favor with the composers of succeeding generations.

Compare Jos. W. I, 70,2,5; 84,2,1; M. I, 76,4,1; 101,5,+2; Genet (Amb. V), 217,4,+2; 224,1,+2; de Orto (Amb. V), 199,2,+2; H. Fink (Amb. V), 261,5,+1; 272,1,1; Stolzer (Amb. V), 290,2,+2; Isaac (Amb.V), 352,2,3; 352,4,1; 360,2,+1; 360,4,1; de Orto (Amb.V), 197,2,+2.

Other combinations occur even more frequently as the initial chord in the formula:

It should be noted that in the above examples the fourth is usually approached in conjunct motion. Occasionally, however, it is introduced by skip: Jos. W. I, 85,3,4; and M. I, 86,1,+1.

Sometimes the six-five combination resolves to a six-four chord when the latter is only a quarter note in duration and unaccented.

---

[6] In which the formula is used with distinct modulatory significance.

Jos. M. I, 40,5,+4.                    Jos. M. I, 74,4,2.

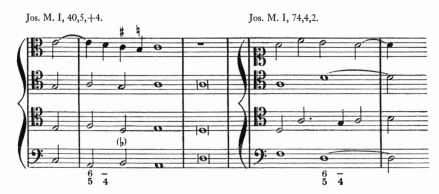

The six-four combination also occurs in various more or less incidental situations over a sustained bass.

Jos. M. I, 64,2,+3.                    Jos. M. I, 64,3,1.

Compare further Jos. W. I, 82,4,1; Jos. M. I, 64,2,3; 64,2,+1; 87,2,+1; A. Brumel (Amb. V), 172,3,3; de Orto (Amb. V), 194,2,3; 195,2,3; Genet (Amb. V), 222,3,3; 222,4,+3; Fink (Amb. V), 270,2,+2; 279,1,+1.

II-B. *The passing six-four chord*

This type continues in many variations, often with distinct harmonic effect.

Jos. W. I, 72,4,3.          Jos. M. I, 47,5,5.          Jos. W. I., 47,3,+2.

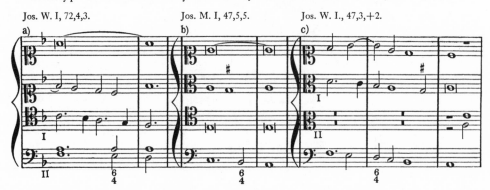

The example *c* is exceptional in that such a six-four chord is more usually resolved by step in the upper voice over a stationary bass.

Compare Jos. M. I, 50,4,+1; 55,4,2; 71,5,+1; Agricola (Amb. V), 181,4,1; Genet (Amb. V), 219,4,+2.

The following is also unusual:

Jos. W. I, 71,1,+1.

Compare de Orto (Amb. V), 199,3,+1.

With the fourth more as a passing note in an upper part:

Jos. M. I, 92,3,1.

Compare further Jos. M. I, 79,4,+2; 89,3,+1; 104,2,1; 107,2,5; 116,4,+2; 126,4,3; 136,4, +1; 148,2,+1; Layolle (Amb. V), 206,1,2; 206,1,+1; Genet (Amb. V), 213,4,2; 216,2,4; Fink (Amb. V), 271,2,+1; 273,4,+2; Isaac (Amb. V), 354,2,+1.

Six-four combinations resulting from the use of extended auxiliary notes in an upper part or in the bass:

Jos. M. I, 75,5,+1.          Jos. M. I, 15,4,3.          Jos. M. I, 15,4,+2.

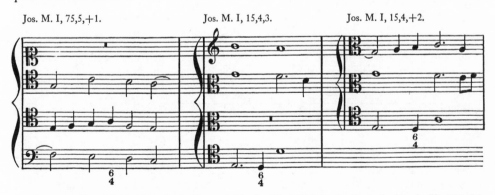

Compare Jos. M. I, 150,3,3; A. Brumel (Amb. V), 154,2,1; A. Agricola (Amb. V), 182,5,1.

Or of changing notes or anticipation:

Jos. M. I, 40,4,4.　　　　　Jos. M. I, 47,1,3.　　　　　Jos. M. I, 100,5,+1.

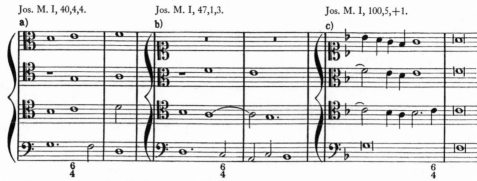

In example *a* the six-four enters through the syncopation in the bass but the *f* in the bass against the *g* and *e* in the two upper parts cannot be a note of resolution; hence, with the relatively long value of the notes in the upper voices (which in shorter time values might be more clearly passing notes), the chord character of the six-four combination is enhanced.

To *b*, compare Jos. M. I, 117,2,+1; 135,2,+2.　　　To *c*, compare Jos. M. I, 102,4,3.
See further La Rue (Amb. V), 138,1,2; Genet (Amb. V), 218,5,+2.

These instances are quite obviously the result of various ornamental devices, but their continual recurrence must have had some influence in the conception of the combination in its vertical aspect as a more or less independent chordal possibility. Consider for example the first six-four chord in the illustration Jos. W. I, 11,2,+1.[7] Here the six-four chord is treated quite freely in the leap to and from the bass note and in the skip to the fourth in the next to the top part.

## II-c. *The arpeggio six-four chord*

The following examples show treatments of the six-four chord which a more modern theorist, such as Riemann or Thuille, would undoubtedly classify as the second inversion of the particular triad involved. That it was not so named or designated in the period under consideration does not, for the moment, enter into the question.

Jos. W. I, 58,4,3.　　　　　Jos. W. I, 37,2,+3.　　　　　Jos. M. I, 99,3,+2.

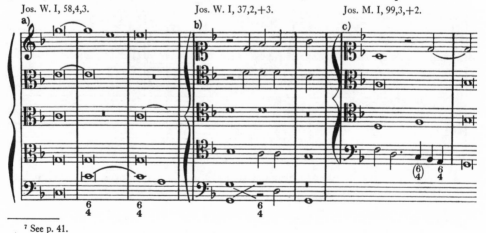

[7] See p. 41.

To *b*, compare Jos. W. I, 81,2,2; Jos. M. I, 74,3,4; A. Agricola (Amb. V), 181,2,1; 182,4,2.

The passage in the lowest part in example *c* is analogous to the common occurrence in instrumental music where the right hand holds the notes of a triad while the bass has running passages of scales or arpeggios in which the fifth of the chord as well as the root and the third is treated freely as what moderns would call an essential note or a chord constituent.

That so many pages and even whole compositions were written wherein no six-four combination appeared, certainly substantiates the idea that the five-three and six-three chords provided the "essential" material for the composers of the Netherland Schools. The occurrence of the six-four combination in phrases and particularly in cadence formulae, with the common treatment of the fourth as a dissonance, even if only of a mild sort (often serving as the preparation for a stronger syncope dissonance), and on the other hand, the occasional freer treatment of the fourth—these are factors which must be reckoned with in any discussion of the possibility of including the six-four chord with the "essential" material. The doubtful standing of the fourth—now as a consonance and again as a dissonance—theoretically one of the simple consonant intervals and yet practically, especially above the bass, usually of a frankly dissonant character—this has been the troublesome question for many generations.

This period is of great significance in the evolution of the six-four chord. Crude and ineffective practices of the earlier composers tend to fall into disuse and the more refined and effective idioms survive. Thus, for example, the accented prepared six-four tends to be associated more frequently with a cadence formula on the fifth degree of the scale; the accented unprepared six-four practically disappears; and the $\left\{ \begin{smallmatrix} 6\text{--}5 \\ 43\text{--} \end{smallmatrix} \right.$ formula gives way to the $\left\{ \begin{smallmatrix} 65\text{--} \\ 4\text{--}3 \end{smallmatrix} \right.$ as the favored cadential procedure.

# CHAPTER VI

## THE EARLY SIXTEENTH CENTURY

IN THE PERIOD between Josquin and Palestrina a great number of composers were active. Prominent in any list of representatives of this time is the name of Nicolaus Gombert.[1] In his works the harmonic feeling which was obviously growing in the 15th century and which showed itself most distinctly in the cadence formula, continued to develop, and at the same time increasing care was shown in the treatment of the dissonance.

I-A. *The accented (or semi-accented), prepared six-four chord*

The $\overset{6-}{\underset{43}{\smile}}$ is comparatively infrequent:

Gom. T. M. 1878 P, 28,2,+2.

Here the six-four occurs on the fourth degree of the scale with respect to the cadence. The form $\overset{5-}{\underset{43}{\smile}}$ continues to be much preferred in the cadence formula.

The following example shows the $\overset{6-}{\underset{43}{\smile}}$ followed by the skip of the fourth in the bass:

Gom. T. M. 1884 R, 20,3,+2.

Compare B. Ducis (Amb. V), 241,2,2; Gombert (Amb. V), 226,3,1.

---

[1] Maldéghem, R. J. van, *Trésor Musical* (Brussels, 1865–1893), "Musique Religieuse" (1866), p. 46, writes: "On peut sans crainte donner à Gombert le titre glorieux de novateur et de modèle de son époque, de précurseur du style Palestrina, pour avoir produit un grand nombre de compositions qui peuvent être mises en parallèle avec celles de l'immortel prince des musiciens d'Italie." Compare Amb., 3: 298; Riemann, *Hdb. d. MG.*, 2, pt. 1: 301; and Adler-Orel, p. 327.

The $^{65}_{43}$ occurs frequently followed by cadential skip of a fourth up or a fifth down, but seldom in the final cadence. More often it is to be found either in some sort of intermediate cadence or in the course of a phrase.

Gom. T. M. 1866 R, 5,3,2.

Here it occurs in the course of the phrase—the chord to which the combination progresses is a chord of the sixth.

Gom. T. M. 1878 P, 26,2,2.

Compare B. Ducis (Amb. V), 235,3,1; 236,3,+1; 242,3,1; 243,3,3.

Very often the bass note is the last note of the phrase in that part and the *effect* only of a progression of a fourth up is produced by the treatment of the other parts.

Gom. T. M. 1878 P, 21,2,2    Gom. T. M. 1878 P, 26,2,+2/1.

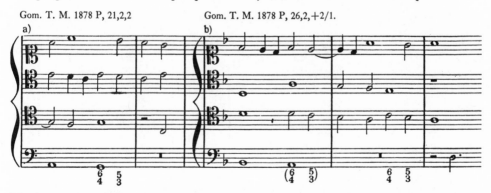

The latter example illustrates the doubtful position of the six-four chord in its cadential significance among composers of the early 16th century.

Several notes may be made:

1. The frequency with which this six-four formula occurs over the last note in a phrase in the bass shows perhaps an early stage of the use of the six-four in a sort of half-cadence or plagal cadence relation.

2. The fact that in the resolution of the first six-four the third of the five-three is minor, and in the last $_{43}^{65}$ the fifth, according to the signature, is diminished,[2] shows that the attitude of the period toward the use of the six-four in direct cadential connections was, in a modern sense, quite undeveloped.

3. In many cadential relations the principles of *musica ficta* would make the third of the five-three, as the leading tone, a major third, but in other cases where the third descended by step forming one type of deceptive cadence it would be major or minor according to the signature.

The following example shows this type of six-four chord used in three different relations in a very short space:

Gom. T. M. 1884 R, 21,5,3.

The first is on the second degree with respect to the final in the common 15th-century manner. The second is on the final itself with the following progression having the effect of a fourth skip to a chord of the sixth. The third six-four chord is on the last note of the phrase in the lowest voice and the succeeding progression is in effect that of a step up in the bass, as in a deceptive cadence progression.

Three further examples are shown:

Gom. T. M. 1881 P, 3,2,+1.    Gom. T. M. 1881 P, 3,2,+3.    Gom. T. M. 1884 R, 22,1,4.

Compare B. Ducis (Amb. V), 241,3,2.

---

[2] In a similar situation Gombert, in T. M. 1881 P,3,2,+1 (quoted on this page) and in other similar places the fifth is made perfect by means of an accidental.

The $^{65}_{43}$ is often followed by a step up in the bass to a six-three or five-three chord. Such an occurrence may frequently be considered as a type of predecessor to the deceptive cadence.

Gom. T. M. 1866 R, 3,2,3.   Gom. T. M. 1866 R, 4,3,+1.   Gom. T. M. 1878 P, 21,2+2.

Compare further Gom. T. M. 1866 R, 3,3,4; 5,3,4; 7,3,+2; 1878 P, 21,4,+3; 25,2,+1; 26,2,+2 (cited on p. 50); 1884 R, 21,5,5 (cited on p. 52); B. Ducis (Amb. V), 236,2,+1; 241,2,3.

That such progressions had an exclusive $^{I-V-VI}_{\substack{6\ 5 \\ 4\ 3}}$ or $^{I-V-IV}_{\substack{6\ 5\ 6 \\ 4\ 3}}$ effect can scarcely be maintained. It would be more accurate to say that this effect occasionally occurred and in time came to be preferred to a similar progression on other degrees of the scale.[3]

The $^{65}_{43}$ was also followed by the progression, a step down in the bass. Sometimes this is the effect of a $^{65}_{43}$ on the second degree before the final:

Gom. T. M. 1884 R, 21,5,3.

sometimes on the fifth degree like a $\begin{array}{c|c} I\ V & IV \\ 6\ 5 & \\ 4\ 3 & \end{array}$ or similar progression:

Gom. T. M. 1866 R, 3,1,+1.              Gom. T. M. 1866 R, 6,3,1.

[3] Even in Palestrina, for example see p. 63, the effect was occasionally that of a $^{65}_{43}$ progression on the fourth degree of the scale followed by a movement of a step up to the V.

sometimes as if on the sixth degree before a dominant chord:

and sometimes in relations that are more difficult to classify tonally:

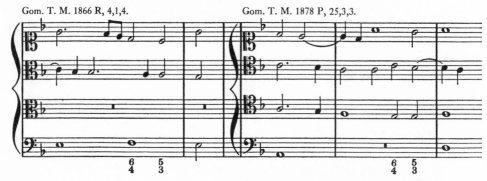

I-B. *The accented (or semi-accented), unprepared six-four chord*

For this type no examples have been found.[4]

II-A. *The auxiliary six-four chord*

In the Gombert examples the auxiliary six-four is the most common of the unaccented types. It occurs usually in an obvious cadence-like formula in which the $\left\{ \begin{smallmatrix} 65- \\ 4-3 \end{smallmatrix} \right.$ is followed by a skip of a fourth up or a fifth down.

Compare Gom. T. M. 1866 R, 6,3,+2; B. Ducis (Amb. V), 238,3,+2; 245,1,+2; Senfl (Amb. V), 402,1,2.

[4] See p. 44.

This combination, $\{^{65-}_{4-3}$, is also followed by the progression of a step up in the bass in a sort of deceptive cadence formula:

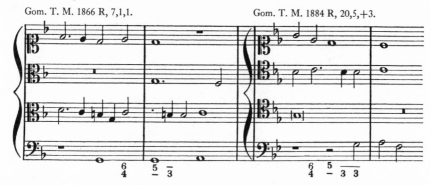

and also without either of these relations in which case it is probably more like the auxiliary six-four which later occurs over the stationary bass of a final chord:

Compare Senfl (Amb. V), 394,1,+1; 402,4,2.

## II-B. *The passing six-four chord*

The passing six-fours of the various types are much less frequent but they still continue to occur—chiefly, however, as accidental phenomena.

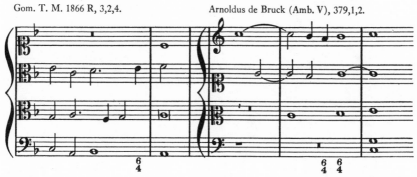

Compare further Gom. T. M. 1866 R, 4,2,2; 5,3,3; Gombert (Amb. V), 225,2,+1; D. Kohler (Amb. V), 365,2,+2.

In the following example the *g* in the bass is quitted in a changing note combination as if it were considered as a consonant.

Gom. T. M. 1884 R, 21,1,2.

II-c. *The arpeggio six-four chord*

For this type no examples have been found.[5]

This period shows a continued development in the various aspects of the use of the six-four chord, particularly with regard to the increasing care in the treatment of the dissonance and in the crystallization of the most effective cadence formulae. The ground is fully prepared for the composers of the next generation, so that Palestrina and his contemporaries could now devote themselves to the final perfecting of that style for which the 16th century is most noted in the history of music.

---

[5] See p. 74.

# CHAPTER VII

## THE PALESTRINA PERIOD

PALESTRINA'S WORKS mark the culmination of a great period in the history of music. His treatment of the dissonance has been the subject of a thorough-going research in the outstanding work of Jeppesen. His care in the use of dissonance can scarcely be questioned. His treatment of the six-four chord should therefore be accepted as the authoritative and decisive standard of the period.

### I-A. *The accented (or semi-accented), prepared six-four chord*

The $\underset{43}{6-}$ type of resolution of the six-four chord is found with relative infrequency. It still occurs, but usually in situations reminiscent of the 15th-century procedures.

P. I, 121,3,1.    P. I, 123,2,5.    P. IV, 3,2,1.

Compare P. V, 156,3,3.

By far the most common use of the accented six-four chord in Palestrina is in the $\underset{43}{65}$ formula.

The usual procedure is for the bass to move by the skip of the fourth up or of the fifth down. That Palestrina appreciated the value of such a formula in a final cadence seems beyond all doubt.

P. VIII, 56,3,+2.

It must not be inferred, however, that this was a favorite device of Palestrina or that he frequently used it in the final cadence in a composition or a movement. Even with the skip of the fourth up or of the fifth down from the bass of the five-three chord, it is most commonly found in an intermediate cadence or in a cadence-like progression in the course of a phrase.

Compare P. VII, 198,2,2; P. VIII, 75,4,+4.

This shows a solid $\underset{43}{65}$ cadence on the dominant but it is an intermediate, not a final cadence.

P. V, 32,3,2.

Compare P. I, 15,1,3; 15,1,+2; 15,2,1; 16,1,1; P. II, 5,2,4; 158,2,2 (in seven parts); P. V, 174,3,+4; P. VI, 30,3,+1; P. VII, 86,2,+2; P. VIII, 146,3,+2; 147,1,1; 147,1,2; 147,1,4; P. IX, 206,2,+3; P. X, 3,4,3; 55,4,+3; 85,4,1; 119,3,+4; P. XI, 7,3,2; 7,3,+3; etc.

The effect of the progression with the skip of the fourth up, was often produced without the movement actually taking place in the bass.[1]

---

[1] See p. 51.

A few of the many similar instances may be cited: P. I, 15,1,2; 23,2,4; 25,2,+1; 29,2,+1; 51,1,2; 55,3,+2; 87,2,3; 109,2,+3; 109,2,+1; 109,3,2; 115,3,+3; 131,1,1; 131,1,+3; P. II, 3,2,1; 51,3,+1; 75,1,+1; P. V, 7,3,+1; 7,4,+1; 8,1,+2; 28,4,+2; P. VI, 30,3,+2; P. VIII, 1,2,3; P. IX, 15,1,1; 109,3,+2; P. X, 137,3,+3; P. XI, 12,4,+2; 44,3,+1; 44,4,4; etc.

Palestrina also occasionally used a device familiar to 15th-century procedure, i.e., a $\overset{65}{\underset{43}{\smallsmile}}$ which involved the crossing of the tenor and bass.

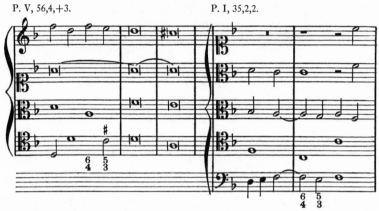

P. V, 56,4,+3.                                   P. I, 35,2,2.

Compare P. VIII, 32,4,1.

The following examples are worth noting and suggestive of the viewpoint in the 16th century with respect to the relation of the accented six-four chord to the cadence. They imply, for instance, that the $\left.\overset{5-}{\underset{43}{\smallsmile}}\right|$ as the stronger dissonance was still felt to be more desirable in the final close,[2] whereas the $\overset{65}{\underset{43}{\smallsmile}}$, although dissonant and somewhat cadential in effect, was still decidedly influenced by a modal point of view.

P. VIII, 139,2,+3.                              P. X, 55,4,+3.

Compare P. V, 35,4,4; P. IX, 105,1,+3; P. X, 60,2,+3; P. XI, 44,2,+3.

In many of the examples, the $\overset{65}{\underset{43}{\smallsmile}}$ may be considered as a prototype, at least, of the modern accented six-four chord as used in a half-cadence $\left(\begin{smallmatrix} \text{I} & \text{V} \\ 6 & 5 \\ & 4 & 3 \end{smallmatrix}\right)$ or as it appears in the plagal decoration of the tonic $\left(\begin{smallmatrix} \text{IV} & \text{I} \\ 6 & 5 \\ 4 & 3 \end{smallmatrix}\right)$ in a final cadence.

---

[2] See p. 50.

The following will illustrate the point:

P. V, 55,2,+4.                                           P. VIII, 1,3,4.

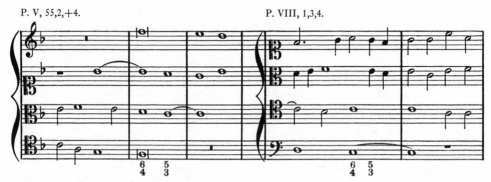

Compare P. I, 3,3,3; 8,3,+2; 16,1,1/2; 17,2,+3; 21,2,1; 123,1,+2; 127,3,+4; P. V, 4,3,+1; 10,4,3; 35,4,4; P. VIII, 87,2,+3; 143,4,+1; 144,3,+1; 144,4,3; P. IX, 37,2,3; P. X, 5,3,+4; 7,3,+3; 69,4,+4; 174,1,1; P. XI, 3,3,1; 44,3,+2, etc.

Made up of a combination of these procedures, cadences like the following are highly interesting:

P. VIII, 172,1,+3.

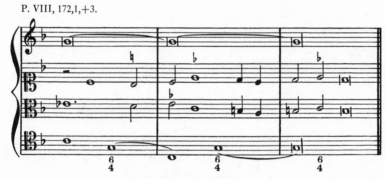

Two further excerpts are quoted, which are worth studying in relation to the foregoing.

P. I, 74,2,+3.                                           P. VIII, 32,4,+4.

Compare P. V, 6,3,+3; P. VIII, 59,4,+3; 88,3,+2; 116,4,+2; 172,1,+3; P. X, 104,3,+3.

It would be expected that, as the cadential force of the accented $\underset{43}{65}$ came to be felt more clearly, it would be used in connection with modulatory passages. That Palestrina was aware of such possibilities is evidenced by such treatments as the following:

P. VI, 30,3,+2.                                    P. I, 15,1,2.

Compare further P. I, 15,1,+2; 15,2,1; P. I, 109,2,+3; 109,2,+1; 109,3,2; P. VI, 30,3,+2/1; P. VIII, 146,3,+1; 147,1,1; 147,1,2; 147,1,4; P. XI, 7,3,2; 7,3,5; etc., etc.

The accented $\underset{43}{65}$ is often followed by the step of a second (actually or in effect) upward in the bass, sometimes producing a deceptive cadence effect.

P. V, 26,2,2.

P. I, 11,1,5.                                    P. I, 17,1,+2.

Compare further P. I, 8,3,+1; 10,3,3; 11,1,+3; 11,2,4; 15,2,2; 127,3,4; 147,2,2; P. III, 111,3,+1; P. V, 4,3,2; P. VI, 13,2,4; 16,2,2; P. VIII, 1,3,2; 141,1,3; 141,2,1; 142,1,+2; 145,4,5; 146,3,2; 148,1,1; P. IX, 34,3,3; 37,2,+4; 206,2,4; P. X, 174,1,1; P. XI, 2,4,+1; 13,1,4; 14,2,4; P. XV, 11,3,+3.

The effect is also occasionally that of a six-four chord —— $\frac{65}{43}$ —— on the fourth degree of the scale.

P. I, 144,1,3.

P. XV, 35,3,+3.                P. VIII, 31,2,+2.

See also P. V, 20,1,4; 50,4,3; P. XV, 12,2,+1.

At times after this formula $\frac{65}{43}$, the bass proceeds with the direct skip of the fourth down or the fifth up.

P. I, 21,3,1.                        P. I, 11,3,1.

Compare P. VIII, 141,2,5.

The $\underset{43}{65}$ followed by a step down in the bass is characteristic of the period; it is, however, rather to be considered as a leftover as it were from an earlier time.[3] Sometimes it has the effect of $\underset{4}{6}$ $\begin{smallmatrix}I&V\\&\end{smallmatrix}\Big|\begin{smallmatrix}IV\\&\end{smallmatrix}$ :

P. III, 3,2,4.

Compare P. I, 23,2,1; P. VI, 1,2,+2; 30,2,+3; P. VII, 68,3,1; P. VIII, 142,1,+3; 153,4,+2; P. IX, 163,3,+4.

Sometimes it is more like the old fauxbourdon procedure from the Dufay period:

P. V, 6,4,4.

The upper part apparently simply delays in order to avoid the consecutive fifths. Certainly there is little of the cadential six-four effect. Two similar examples are given:

P. V, 7,1,1.                                          P. VIII, 140,2,+1.

[3] See Werner, T. W., "Die Magnificat-Kompositionen A. Rener's," AfMW., 2: 213; Riemann, *Hdb. d. MG.*, 2, pt. 1: 384; and p. 16 of the present work.

Compare further P. I, 6,1,+1; 11,1,+1; 13,3,1; 16,1,2; 17,2,4; P. II, 22,2,4; P. IV, 3,2,1; P. V, 65,3,+3; P. VIII, 142,1,+1; 142,2,2; 143,4,+1; 153,4,+2; P. IX, 3,2,5; 29,2,5; 78,3,2; P. X, 23,1,2; P. XI, 30,5,+3; P. XV, 3,1,1.

At other times it has distinctly the effect of being on the sixth degree of the scale:

P. VIII, 20,1,2.

P. V, 53,4,+2.

P. I, 95,2,4.

P. I, 6,1,+1.

Compare P. I, 13,3,1; 112,3,+1; P. II, 22,2,4; P. IV, 31,2,3; P. V, 8,1,+3; 8,2,3; P. VIII, 71,5,+2; 140,1,+1; P. IX, 78,3,2; P. X, 6,2,+4; 34,2,2; 39,3,4; 66,5,+2; 74,3,+2; 77,2,+3; 128,1,+3; P. XI, 7,2,+2; 33,1,4; 42,2,+2; P. XIII, 1,2,+2; P. XIV, 35,4,+3; 38,2,+2; P. XV, 3,2,1; 3,2,+2; P. XVI, 33,2,+1; XVII, 3,2,1; P. XVIII, 5,1,+2.

When the bass of a $^{65}_{43}$ progression moves downward a third, a six-three chord often occurs on the new bass note. This may be regarded as a derivative variation of the progression in which the bass moves up a fourth or down a fifth. Examples of this, with several interesting variations, are given.

P. VIII, 141,3,1.

P. IX, 35,3,5.

P. VII, 3,2,2.

P. I, 90,2,3.

Compare further P. II, 5,3,2; P. VIII, 143,4,+1; P. IX, 94,2,4; P. X, 7,2,+1; etc.

Such examples as the following are also obviously closely related to the same progression.

P. I, 4,3,2.

P. I, 127, 3,+2.

Compare P. I, 4,3,+4; 10,3,+2.

I-B. *The accented (or semi-accented), unprepared six-four chord*

No examples were found.

II-A. *The auxiliary six-four chord*

It is interesting to note that the pure auxiliary six-four chord, i.e., where the fourth and the sixth are upper auxiliary or returning notes, moving simultaneously in similar motion, occurs much less frequently than the $\left\{{65-\atop4-3}\right.$ formula.

P. VIII, 32,4,+2.                              P. VIII, 172,1,+1.

This movement occurs, of course, in the unaccented portion of the measure. Jeppesen[4] points out that "the fourth was treated as a dissonance by the practical musicians of Palestrina's time." In other words, it was used "almost exclusively in syncopation or as passing dissonance." Jeppesen cites three examples of deviations from the normal mode of treatment and says:[5] "These three instances (as far as my knowledge extends, the only ones found in Palestrina's works), are met with in cadences, and it will be remarked that in them all the dissonance is introduced above a stationary note in the bass."

P. XXV, 122,3,+3.          P. XXV, 59,4,+3.                    P. XXV, 73,3,+3.

---

[4] *Op. cit.*, p. 211.    [5] *Op. cit.*, p. 212.

Jeppesen[6] regards these as the first germs of the pedal dissonance. Significant for the present work is the fact that in every one of the three deviations, the fourth is accompanied by the sixth. Furthermore in:

P. IV, 158,2,3.

*the only place in his whole artistic career where*, according to Jeppesen,[7] Palestrina breaks his laws of style by introducing the passing fourth on the accented beat, the *ascending fourth is accompanied by the sixth*. This is strong evidence that Palestrina was keenly aware of the resonant effect of the six-four combination, and that he considered the six-four which occurred over a stationary bass even on the first beat of the measure as an almost-consonant chord. The "semi-consonant" effect of the fourth over a stationary bass on the unaccented portion of the measure has already been pointed out in connection with the $\left\{ \begin{smallmatrix} 65- \\ 4-3 \end{smallmatrix} \right.$ formula.[8] In this relation it has been called the "consonant fourth,"[9] and here too it is commonly accompanied by the sixth as may be illustrated by the following example:

P. XXV, 18,4,2.

---

[6] *Op. cit.*, p. 212.   [7] *Op. cit.*, p. 251.   [8] See p. 26.

[9] According to Jeppesen (*op. cit.*, p. 212) it was Bellermann who first baptized the fourth thus although Fux had already drawn attention to it (*Gradus*-Mizler, p. 103). Jeppesen traces it back to the earliest masters of the Second Netherland School. The author of the present work (see p. 23) has found a prototype of this form in Binchois. He points out the $-\frac{76-5}{4-3-}-$ as a 15th-century predecessor of it. See also Petrus de Cruce, Wolf III, 5,2,5, cited p. 10 of this work. Compare Albrechtsberger, *Sämtliche Schriften* (ed. 2; Vienna, 1837), 1: 13.

An essential element in this formula is the strong dissonance on the succeeding accent. The rhythmic value of this is obvious. When under similar circumstances both the sixth and the fourth were tied over as in:

P. V, 122,1,+3.

the effect seems to have been considered particularly harsh. Jeppesen,[10] in the section of his book on "Dissonance as a Means of Poetical Expression," points out that the double suspension of the six-four over a stationary bass was mainly used in connection with such somber-colored words as "aspri" (P. XXIX, 181,1,1), "l'empia" (P. XXVIII, 98,3,2), and "crudelis" (P. XXV, 142,1,4; 203,2, +2); and he cites a madrigal in which Palestrina used this combination to symbolize "fallo" (fault).[11]

P. XXIX, 24,2,+2.

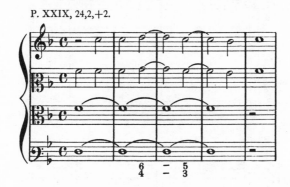

The weakness of the rhythmic effect of the double six-four syncopation in such combinations undoubtedly accounts in large measure for the infrequent occurrence of this procedure. Similarly in the following,

---

[10] *Op. cit.*, p. 254.

[11] This, to the author's knowledge, is the first instance in which there is evidence that the six-four chord is used for purposes of "poetic expression." See Hedwig Pospischil, "Untersuchungen über die psychologischen Wirkungen der Lagenverhältnisse" (Diss.; Wien, 1928).

P. XII, 50,4,1.                    P. XII, 69,4,+1.

the rhythmic effect is weak compared with the $\begin{Bmatrix} 65- \\ 4-3 \end{Bmatrix}$, and such occurrences are rare in Palestrina.

Compare P. VII, 66,2,+2; VIII, 107,1,+2.

As has already been said,[12] the auxiliary six-four in Palestrina occurs most commonly in the familiar cadential formula $\begin{Bmatrix} 65- \\ 4-3 \end{Bmatrix}$. The fourth as a dissonance is treated almost invariably in conjunct motion, either as an upper auxiliary or descending passing note, but seldom as an ascending passing note save in conjunction with another part which makes the usual resolution.

P. VII, 106,2,2.

P. I, 114,3,2.

---

[12] See p. 67.

In Palestrina the $\left\{ \begin{smallmatrix} 65-\\ 4-3 \end{smallmatrix} \right.$ formula is used:

1. In a perfect cadence at the end of a phrase:

P. I, 24,1,+3.

P. I, 17,3,3.

P. III, 9,2,+2.

Compare P. I, 11,1,3; 24,1,+3; 106,3,1; 107,3,3; 114,3,2; 117,3,3; P. II, 51,1,+2; 62,2,+4; P. III, 7,3,+4; 15,2,+3; P. IV, 3,2,5; 69,3,+3; P.V, 70,4,3; 96,4,+3; P.VI, 21,3,+2; 31,2,+3; P. VII, 57,2,+2; 107,2,2; 110,2,3; 115,2,4; 198,1,+2; P. VIII, 17,2,+2; 23,4,+2; 30,2,+2; 41,3,+2; 46,3,+2; 77,3,+2; 93,4,+2; 121,3,+2; 129,2,+2; 142,2,+3; 145,2,+2; P. XI, 18,4,+2; P. XIII, 45,4,+2; P. XVI, 63,3,+2; etc.

2. In a perfect cadence formula in the course of a phrase:

P. I, 9,3,4.                                    P. I, 11,1,3.

Further examples may be found among the citations given in the preceding group; the overlapping phrasing characteristic of the Palestrina style does not permit of a rigid distinction between these two types.

3. In a situation not unlike some sort of deceptive cadence, often in the course of a phrase. The prevailing use of the modal system allows or brings about many effects characteristic of that system and foreign to the modern major and minor practice.

P. V, 7,3,3.                                    P. I, 122,2,4.

Out of a great number the following examples may be cited: P. I, 57,2,+4; P. VIII, 1,2,+1; 127,4,+4; 138,3,+1; 157,4,4; P. X, 9,2,+3.

The interweaving of the parts in Palestrina is such that, as is well known, as one part progresses to a close before a rest, other parts continue or new parts enter, so that the effect as a whole is continuous—there is no break. Often in these situations the usual cadence formulae are used except that, through this interweaving treatment of the parts, no break is perceptible. These "overlapping" phrases are common in Palestrina, and in such situations the six-four chord often occurs. The following examples, one with a double chorus, will illustrate the point:

P. VI, 69,2,2.

P. I, 134,2,3.

Compare P. X, 9,2,2; 9,2,+3; P. XVII, 43,3,1, as well as many of the preceding examples.

## II-B. *The passing six-four chord*

The passing six-fours continue to appear in Palestrina in various forms but with a restraint in the treatment of the fourth which is characteristic. The following examples will serve as illustrations.

P. I, 121,3,+4.

P. XV, 71,4,+2.    P. XV, 72,2,+3.    P. XI, 16,1,2.    P. XI, 15,4,+3.

## II-C. *The arpeggio six-four chord*

Clear-cut examples of this type are as difficult to find in Palestrina as in the other vocal music of the 16th century. The type seems quite definitely to have its origin in instrumental music. The following examples, however, are suggestive:

P. XI, 99,1,+2.

The first, Jeppesen[13] classes under "accentual alteration." This example and the next are strong evidence that Palestrina was aware of the *effect* of the six-four chord as what in a later period was termed the second inversion of a triad, although he probably did not employ that terminology for it. The skip of the octave to the fourth in P. XI, 66,1,+2 is the factor which shows how close Palestrina must have come to the idea of chord inversion in connection with the six-four chord—the *g* in the middle voice simply sustains until, with the octave skip of the bass, it finds itself suddenly, but about as imperceptibly as possible, doing duty as the bass.

P. XI, 66,1,+2.

Following the evolution of the six-four chord through the works of Palestrina, we find that he treats the dissonance with characteristic restraint. With regard to the relation of the six-four to the cadence, remnants of earlier procedures are to be found but usages of a more modern type greatly predominate. The accented prepared six-four in the $\underset{43}{65}$ formula and the auxiliary six-four in the $\{\underset{4-3}{65-}$ formula, both on the fifth degree of the scale, are the most usual types. In the works discussed in the following chapters, the freer treatments of the dissonance, which have completely disappeared in Palestrina, begin to appear again but in new forms and under new conditions.

---

[13] *Op. cit.*, p. 251.

# CHAPTER VIII

# MONTEVERDI

Monteverdi's position in the History of Music at the turning of the 16th century makes imperative a study of his use of the six-four chord. Hugo Leichtentritt[1] says:

Als Madrigalist ist Monteverdi eben ein Vollender, ähnlich wie Bach in der Suite, der Fuge, Beethoven in der Sonata; als Opernkomponist ist er ein Bahnbrecher. Die Historie wird auch dem Opernkomponisten Monteverdi Unsterblichkeit zugestehen müssen, die lebendige Kunst-übung wird sich an die Madrigale halten müssen.

Henry Prunières[2] says, of the *Second Book of Madrigals* (1590),[3]

Certains madrigaux ont une forme polyphonique très accentuée, d'autres au contraire sont écrits en style homophone, en accords verticaux. On sent que l'auteur n'est pas un homme à théorie mais avant tout un musicien suivant son inspiration ou son caprice et se réservant le droit d'observer ou de violer les règles selon son bon plaisir et le résultat à atteindre. Il estime que la fin justifie les moyens et que l'essentiel est de suggérer à l'auditeur avec intensité des sentiments et des impressions.

I-A. *The accented (or unaccented), prepared six-four chord*

The $\underset{43}{65}$ formula in Monteverdi has almost exclusively a cadential bearing. This formation is still preferably used for a cadence occurring in the course of a composition. For the final cadence of a composition, a more elaborate formula is usually preferred. The following examples show typical procedures:

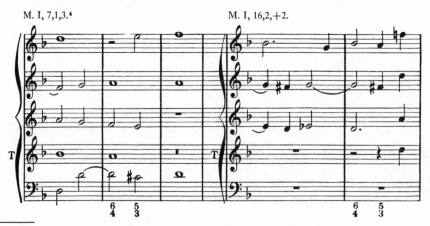

M. I, 7,1,3.[4]    M. I, 16,2,+2.

---

[1] "Claudio Monteverdi als Madrigalkomponist," SIMG, 11 (1910): 256.

[2] *La Vie et l'Oeuvre de Claude Monteverdi* (Paris, 1926), p. 42.

[3] It should be noted that the first three books of madrigals and the three-part *Kanzonetten* (vol. 10) appeared before the death of Palestrina.

[4] Parts marked "T" (tenor) sound an octave lower in the Malipiero edition. In the following examples B means bass and BC, Basso Continuo: the editor's "realizations" of the Basso Continuo are set in small type.

Compare further[5] M. I, 8,3,+4; 21,3,+2; 29,3,1 (B+1); 29,3,+1; 30,1,2; 37,3,3 (B×T); 37,3,+1; 38,3,2 (B×T); 38,3,+2; 40,2,+1; 42,1,2/3; 42,2,2; 42,2,3; 47,1,+2; 48,2,+1; 49,2,1; 59,1,+1; 60,1,+1; 61,1,+2 (B−3 to six-three); 61,2,1; 64,2,+2 (B−1); 68,1,3 (B+1); M. II, 1,2,+2 (B−1); 11,1,3 (B−1); 14,1,+3 (1/2C); 14,2,3 (1/2C); 19,1,1; 22,1,+1 (B+1); 22,2,2 (B+1); 22,2,+2 (B−1); 51,1,+2; 51,2,2 (1/2C); 57,1,+1 (1/2C); 92,3,1 (shows an interesting mixture of new and old procedures, i.e., the addition of the seventh to the five-three chord and the crossing of the tenor and bass parts [compare M. III, 72,1,2]); 94,3,+1; 96,1,+3 (1/2C); 102,2,+2; 102,3,2 (B−3 to six-three); 103,1,+1; 104,1,+2 (B+1); 104,3,+1; 105,3,2 (1/2C); 105,3,+1; 107,1,+1 (B−3 to six-three);

M. II, 93,3,1.

M. III, 3,1,+2 shows the $\underset{43}{65}$ in a half-cadence formula with the new phrase overlapping, giving the effect of a skip of a fourth up in the lowest part.

M. III, 3,1,+2.

[5] Abbreviations used in the following list:

B+1 denotes that the bass moves up by degree following the $\frac{5}{3}$ in a $\underset{43}{65}$ combination,

B−1: bass moves down by step.

B−3 to six-three: bass moves down a third to a six-three chord.

½ C: may be considered as a possible half-cadence effect.

B×T: bass crosses tenor (compare Ziehn, *Harmonie- und Modulationslehre*, p. 61, and *Man. of Harm.*, p. 73).

M. III, 14,3,2 (1/2C); 15,3,1; 23,3,2; 23,3,+1; 25,1,2; 30,1,+2 (B—3 to $\overset{V}{7}$!); 32,1,2; 33,3,+2 (1/2C); 34,1,2 (1/2C); 41,3,2 (minor third in five-three); 42,1,+1; 44,3,1 (1/2C); 45,1,3; 45,3,1 (B+1); 46,1,3.

M. III, 72,1,2.                    M. III, 77,2,+3.

The foregoing examples show the more modern trend of the use of the six-four in Monteverdi.

Compare M. III, 77,3,+2; 84,3,2; 88,2,+2; 94,2,+1; 103,3,2 (combined with suspension of the sixth); 105,3,4 (1/2C); 107,1,2 (B−1); 108,1,1; 108,1,4; M. IV, 2,2,+3 (B+1); 3,1,1; 7,1,+1; 20,1,+1 (B−3 to six-three); 42,3,4 (B+1); 43,1,1 (B+1); 43,1,3 (1/2C); M.V,2,2,1; 3,3,3; 6,2,2 (B+1); 8,1,+3; 26,1,3; 28,2,+1; 31,3,+2; 52,2,+1; 53,3,+2 (1/2C); 59,1,2; 95,1,+1; 100,2,+1; M. VI, 47,2,2; 67,2,+2; etc. (more than 40 examples have been found in the next six volumes).

M. VI, 11,3,+3.

The preceding example, as indicated, occurs in the *Sixth Book of Five-Part Madrigals* (1614). The six-four chord which occurs on the strong accent is rearranged on the second quarter, in that the fourth appears an octave lower in another part where it continues after the manner of the "consonant fourth" spoken of in the preceding chapter.

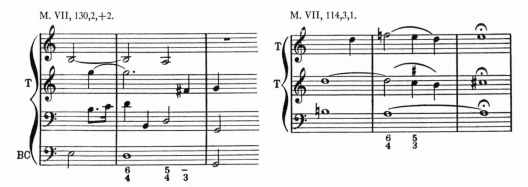

The skip of the tenth in the bass below the Basso Continuo is evidence of the feeling of the six-four as a chord inversion, not merely as a suspension. Note the resolution with a skip of the ninth.

A final cadence in a Symfonia from "Il ritorno d'Ulisse in patria" (1641),

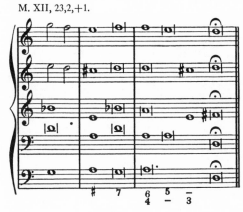

is given as a last example of the use of the accented six-four in a cadence formula by Monteverdi.

The following example from "Orfeo" (1607) is given to show the use of the accented six-four chord in modulation.

M. XI, 43,2,2. ff. Ritornello.

Of course many of the preceding accented six-fours are used in passages effecting modulations. The frequency of the $\underset{43}{65}$ as indicated in the citations given shows the commonness of the use of the tonic six-four chord in actual composition whether the theorists were ready to label it as such or not.

But the $\underset{43}{65}$ was not always used in this relation. Some of the practices of earlier periods continue to appear although less and less frequently. Several examples may be cited.

1. On the sixth degree:

M. III, 29,2,+1.                              M. III, 54,3,1.

In the first example the six-four is of short duration; in the second, the fourth is augmented and the resolution is to a six-three instead of the five-three.

Compare further M. III, 25,2,1; M. VI, 87,1,1.

This example of the six-four on the sixth degree must be regarded as exceptional. It illustrates the difference between Palestrina and Monteverdi, in respect of their point of view regarding the use of the dissonance.

Both of the six-four chords in the following example are unusual in Monteverdi, but they are further illustrative of a changing point of view.

In the first six-four chord, which may be considered as on the sixth degree, the entrance of the fourth by skip in the top voice while it is "prepared" in the next to the lowest part, may be classed in the category which Jeppesen[6] calls "parasitic dissonance." The treatment of the second six-four chord shows how much progress has been made toward a more definite point of view regarding chordal and tonal relationships. Here the chord may be classed with those occurring on the second degree of the scale. The play of the *f* against the *f*-sharp is of course common in the period so that the entire measure may, in modern terms, be explained as derivative of dominant harmonies.

2. On the second degree:

M. III, 106,3,3.

Apart from such passages as this, the $\substack{6-\\43}$ seldom occurs.[7]

---

[6] *Op. cit.*, p. 156.

[7] See for example, M. III, 107,3,1, where the $\substack{6-\\43}$ occurs in the treatment of an interesting chromatic theme:

M. III, 107,3,1.

3. On the fourth degree:

M. I, 21,3,1.

4. On the seventh degree:

Another use of the accented six-four chord in which the prepared fourth may be a diminished interval, occurs in the *First Book of Madrigals* (1587), and with increasing freedom and frequency in the later works. In modern terminology this combination would be described as occurring on the leading tone and resolving on the diminished triad, before passing to the tonic triad.

M. I, 7,1,+1.

Compare M. VII, 88,1,1; 88,1,2; VIII, 45,1,2; 46,1,+2; 47,1,+3; 86,1,2; X, 35,3,1.

5. And even in situations which might be interpreted as on the third degree with relation to the cadence:

M. I, 43,1,4.

M. IX, 15,4,+1.

In Monteverdi the $\underset{43}{65}$ also occurs occasionally in notes of shorter value:

M. I, 65,1,+2.                    M. III, 82,2,3.

Compare M. IV, 11,3,3.

### I-B. *The accented (or semi-accented), unprepared six-four chord*

This also occurs frequently but the parts forming the interval of the fourth usually move in contrary and conjunct motion so that the fourth has the aspect of an accented passing note or an appoggiatura:

Frequently, but not always, these six-four chords have the characteristics of one or another of the cadential forms.

## II-A. *The auxiliary six-four chord*

This group of six-four chords divides distinctly into two classes in Monteverdi, namely, $\begin{Bmatrix} 65 \\ 43 \end{Bmatrix}$ and $\begin{Bmatrix} 65- \\ 4-3 \end{Bmatrix}$. Almost always, the stationary note in the bass may be analyzed as either the fifth or the first degree of the scale.

Examples of the $\begin{Bmatrix} 65 \\ 43 \end{Bmatrix}$ follow:

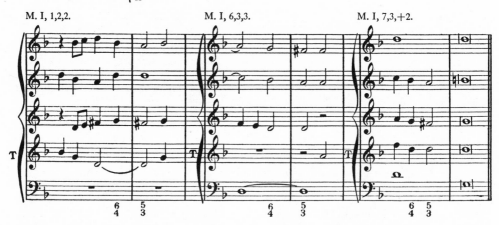

See further M. I, 9,1,+4; 9,1,+1; 11,2,+1; 12,2,1; 15,1,4; 15,2,4; 16,3,3; 17,3,1; 19,3,+2; 20,3,+3; 22,2,4; 29,1,+1; 37,2,3; 38,1,+2; 48,2,1; 58,3,+2; 70,1,1; 70,3,+2; M. II, 19,1,2; 22,3,1; 29,2,1/2; 50,3,2; 57,2,+1; 57,3,3/4; 64,2,1; 64,3,+4; 69,3,3; 86,1,2; 89,1,3/4; 101,1,2; M. III, 10,3,1; 11,1,3; 11,2,1; 20,1,1/2; 34,2,2; 38,3,+1; 39,1,2; 40,1,1; 43,3,1; (continued below).

The inserted examples show variations worth studying.

M. V, 70,2,1.

M. V, 9,2,3.                                M. XI, 71,2,1.

The increasing freedom with which the fourth is treated (approached and quitted by skip, accented as well as unaccented) suggests a growing consciousness of the value and significance of the six-four combination as a chordal entity.

M. III (cont.) 45,1,3; 58,1,3; 61,1,+2; 73,2,1; 79,3,+1; 81,1,+3; 82,2,3; 92,3,+1; 98,2,1; 98,3,+2; 100,2,+2; 104,2,1; 105,3,+1; M. IV, 4,2,1; 6,2,1; 22,3,1; 38,1,3; 39,3,+1; 40,1,+2/1; 56,1,1; 58,3,+3; 61,2,2; 71,3,+2; 77,1,+2; 77,3,+3; 84,2,+2; 86,1,1; 87,1,+1; 99,1,2; 100,3,1; M. V, 4,1,+2; 9,3,1; 10,2,2; 13,3,1; 20,1,2; 23,2,1/2; 23,3,1/2; 23,3,3; 29,1,3; 50,1,+1; 68,1,+2; 72,1,1; M. VI, 6,2,1; 6,3,1; 27,2,+3; 49,3,+3; 58,1,+2; 63,3,1; 63,3,+2; 64,1,1; 64,3,1; 74,1,2; 75,1,3; 86,1,3; 105,1,2/3; 106,1,1; 114,1,4; M. VII, 39,3,+1; 65,3,+1; 67,2,+2; 70,4,+3; 80,4,+3; 92,1,2; 93,1,1; 93,3,+2; 116,3,+1; 122,3,2; 128,3,1/2; 158,1,3; 158,2,+1; M. VIII, 297,1,2; M. IX, 38,3,+2/1; 61,2,+3; 63,1,2; 65,1,+3; 67,1,2; 110,3,2; M. X, 8,1,4; 11,3,+2; 54,4,2; M. XI, 9,4,2 (the six-four is indicated with the figures $\frac{6}{4}$ below the Basso Continuo— "Orfeo," 1609); 73,1,1; 73,1,+1; 73,2,1; 73,2,2; 73,2,+1; 90,2,1; M. XII, 153,1,+2; 154,2,2.

With the use of the Basso Continuo when the chord progression is outlined by the accompanying instrument (Cembalo) the fourth of the six-four chord is used with still greater freedom over the bass.

M. VII, 122,3,1.

Much more common with Monteverdi is the combination $\left\{ \begin{smallmatrix} 65- \\ 4-3 \end{smallmatrix} \right|$. A few typical variations are shown.

M. I, 8,3,+1.                    M. II, 76,3,2.                    M. II, 94,2,+2.

The following list will give an idea of the frequency of this combination:

M. I, 15,1,+1; 17,3,+2; 19,2,1; 20,2,1; 24,1,+1; 24,3,+3; 29,2,1; 32,2,1; 35,3,+2; 36,2,2; 36,2,5; 39,1,+2; 49,1,3; 49,3,+2; 51,2,2; 55,2,2; 55,2,+1; 55,3,2; 56,3,1; 56,3,+2; 57,1,1; 57,3,+2; 58,2,2; 59,3,+2; 60,3,+2; 61,2,1; M. II, 2,1,1; 2,2,+1; 4,3,+1; 5,1,4; 10,3,+2; 14,3,+3; 17,2,2; 18,3,+2; 19,1,3; 20,2,2; 22,3,2; 23,3,+3/2; 25,1,+2; 26,2,3; 26,2,+1; 27,3,+1; 28,3,+3; 31,1,1; 32,3,+1; 33,2,+1; 34,1,3; 38,1,3; 48,3,+2; 51,2,+1; 52,3,+2; 53,3,3; 54,3,3; 56,2,+2; 57,2,1; 57,3,1; 64,2,2; 64,3,+3; 66,2,3; 68,3,2; 70,1,2; 70,3,1; 72,1,1; 74,3,+3; 84,2,+3; 86,3,+2; 87,3,+2; 88,1,+1; 90,2,2; 91,3,+3; 93,2,1; 93,3,+2; 94,2,+2; 94,3,3; 95,1,1; 96,3,+3; 99,1,1; 100,2,1; 100,3,+1; 101,2,+2; 101,3,3; 101,3,+3; 107,3,+2; M. III, 1,2,1; 3,3,1; 4,2,1; 5,1,1; 5,1,+2; 6,2,+2; 6,3,3; 7,1,+2; 7,3,+2; 12,1,3; 12,3,+3; 14,2,+2; 17,3,4; 17,3,+2; 18,3,+3; 21,1,2; 21,3,+3; 22,1,3; 24,3,2; 25,3,+3; 26,3,3; 27,1,3; 27,1,+1; 27,2,+3; 30,1,1; 32,2,2; 37,2,2; 38,2,1; 40,3,+2;

M. III (Cont.) 47,3,+2; 50,1,+1; 50,2,+1; 54,1,2; 54,2,+2; 54,3,2; 61,3,+3; 67,3,+3; 68,3,1; 69,1,3; 70,3,2; 71,2,1; 72,3,1; 73,2,2; 75,2,1; 75,3,+2; 77,1,+1; 77,3,1; 83,1,2; 83,3,1; 85,3,3; 86,1,3; 86,3,+3; 91,2,+2; 91,3,+2; 92,3,3; 93,3,2; 94,3,+3; 96,1,3; 98,1,1; 105,3,3; 108,1,+3; 109,2,+3; 110,3,+2; 113,3,2; M. IV, 2,1,3; 3,2,+2; 5,1,1; 6,1,+1 (an interesting variation in which the six-four is followed by a six-five instead of the usual five-four combination); 6,2,2; 6,3,1; 19,3,+3; 33,1,+1; 34,1,+1; 34,3,1; 34,3,+3; 37,3,2; 37,3,+1; 38,2,3; 38,2,+1; 38,3,3; 39,2,+1; 40,1,2; 40,3,1; 40,3,+2; 43,2,4; 48,3,+3; 52,3,3; 53,1,2; 53,2,2; 53,3,+3; 60,3,+2; 65,3,+2; 67,3,+2; 69,2,2; 73,1,+1; 74,3,1; 75,3,2; 76,2,+2; 76,3,1; 77,1,3; 77,2,1; 80,2,3; 83,3,+2; 85,1,2; 86,3,+3; 87,3,+2; 89,3,+2; 90,1,+2; 90,3,1/2; 95,2,2; 95,3,+3; 97,3,+2; 99,1,3; 101,1,2; 101,2,+2; 102,2,1; 102,3,+3; M. V, 10,1,+1; 24,2,+2; 25,1,+1; 46,3,+2; 61,3,+2; 66,1,2; 86,1,1; 86,1,+2; 87,2,3; 96,2,1; 99,2,1;

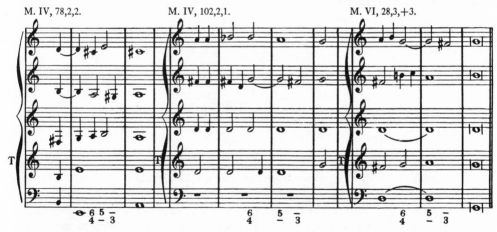

M. VI, 1,2,+2; 3,3,+2; 11,2,3; 11,3,+2; 13,3,1; 20,2,+2; 21,3,+3; 28,3,+3; 32,1,+1; 32,2,+2; 33,2,+3; 44,1,2; 44,2,2; 49,3,+3; 56,3,+2; 59,3,2; 60,2,+2; 60,3,1; 61,2,2; 61,3,+1; 69,3,+2; 78,2,3; 80,2,+2; 87,1,2; 106,2,2; 112,2,+2; M. VII, 9,1,1; 11,4,1; 13,2,+2; 17,1,+1; 20,3,3; 36,2,2; 38,2,2; 40,4,+3; 48,1,1; 48,1,2; 48,2,1; 54,4,+3; 57,1,2; 68,1,3; 70,2,+2; 70,4,+2; 74,2,2; 76,3,3; 77,3,+2; 78,4,2; 78,4,+2; 80,4,+2; 81,2,+1; 93,2,1; 95,1,1; 96,2,3; 97,3,+2;

103,2,+2; 103,3,+3; 116,3,3; 117,2,+2; 122,3,+3; 124,2,2; 127,3,1; 128,3,2; 134,3,3; 141,1,2; 155,3,+3; 157,2,1; 157,4,+3; M. VIII, 44,1,2; 44,1,+1; 56,1,+3; 95,4,+3; 105,2,2; 184,1,+3; 203,1,+3; 211,1,2; 221,1,2; 248,1,2; 263,4,+2; 300,3,2; 331,3,1; 331,3,+2; M. IX, 19,4,2/4; 31,2,2;

31,4,+2; 33,4,3; 38,2,1; 38,2,3; 96,1,+2; 97,2,+1; 104,1,1; 105,4,1; 108,1,1; M. X, 14,1,+2; 15,3,+2; 23,1,+1; 23,4,+2; M. XI, 35,1,+1; 37,3,1; 39,2,+2; 71,3,+1; 150,1,1; M. XII, 29,3,2; 29,4,2; 30,4,1; 39,3,+1; 126,1,+1.

In connection with this particular cadence formula $\left(\left\{\begin{smallmatrix} 65- \\ 4-3 \end{smallmatrix}\right\}\right)$ one has an illustration of a very fundamental psychological principle in the development of dissonance treatment. For example, when a formula like this is used so many, many times, it seems inevitable that one would grow tired of it, and crave variation, novelty, anything to gain relief from the barrenness of the constant repetition of a set formula. When the harmonic background is thus clearly fixed, it is natural that greater complication should be sought. How was this to be obtained? Simply by a skillful introduction of a new dissonance together with certain rhythmic elaboration.[8] Such simple variations as the fol-

---

[8] To follow this idea through all its ramifications would lead too far from our present purpose. It would, however, make an excellent topic for an independent study, for from just such situations, new harmonic possibilities may arise.

lowing, which are very similar to certain 15th-century procedures, produce what would
be classified in modern harmony as the first inversion of the augmented triad.

The following treatment of the dissonance is probably best understood in this light,

while such situations as the following must have aided in the crystallization of the
concept of the higher dominant dissonances.

---

[9] In this example the six-four chord as such does not appear, but the relation to the formula momentarily under
consideration is obvious. In this connection compare M. IV, 44,2,+2.

In other variations the fourth and sixth are both suspended against the fifth, which gives another "heaping up" of dissonance, for which Monteverdi has become famous.

Compare further M. IV, 33,2,+1; 38,1,+1; 43,2,2; M. V, 4,1,3.

The following may also be accepted as variations:

Compare M. V, 60,2,+3; 61,1,+2.

M. VI, 10,2,+2 is another example of Monteverdi's flare for innovation in that the suspended fourth in the bass, instead of resolving to a mere diminished fifth as was the common procedure in the 16th century,[10] resolves on a diminished seventh which in turn is freely but logically treated.

Other variations of this formula, which occur with other chords than the six-four, are discussed by Jeppesen.[11]

The six-four chord itself may be more or less an incidental constituent of the formula. But the frequency with which it does appear in a clear-cut fashion, as indicated by the numerous examples already cited, certainly cannot be ignored as an important factor in the preparation of the necessary psychological attitude toward it so that, when the idea of chord inversion did develop, it could readily be classed as the second inversion of a triad.

Like the other cadential formulae, this was often used by Monteverdi with modulatory significance. One or two examples will suffice to illustrate the procedure:

The second example is particularly interesting and worth studying in the context.

Compare further M. III, 30,1,+1; M. IV, 76,2,+2; 76,3,1.

---

[10] Compare Jeppesen, *op. cit.*, p. 225.     [11] *Op. cit.*, pp. 219 ff.

II-B. *The passing six-four chord*

This chord continues to appear in various forms and in different relations to the accent as the following examples show.

M. II, 25,2,2.

See further M. II, 27,3,3; 27,3,+3; 28,2,1/2; M. III, 32,3,1; M. IX, 11,4,2; 12,3,2; 15,4,2; 39,4,+3.

M. II, 50,2,+3.

M. VII, 189,2,3.

Compare M. III, 7,2,+2; IV, 2,2,+2; V, 78,2,1.

M. X, 54,2,+1.

M. III, 10,2,+1.          M. III, 22,3,1.

See also M. III, 11,1,2; 50,1,1; M. V, 98,1,1.

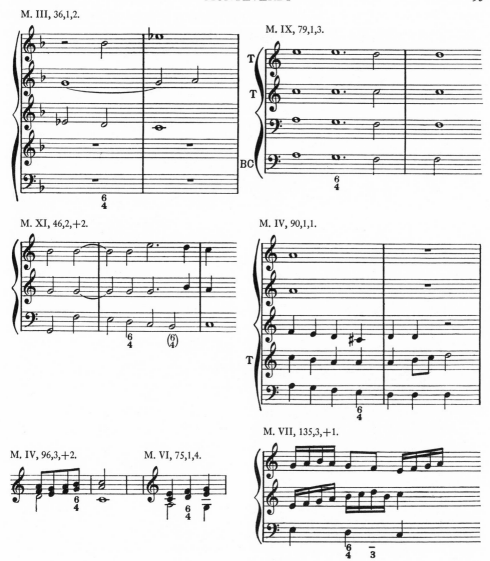

A freer form occurs through the use of the extended auxiliary or the anticipation, but the six-four chords from such combinations are not so frequent in Monteverdi as in the 15th-century composers.

See also M. V, 67,2,+1; M. VI, 71,3,+1; M. VII, 116,1,1; M. IX, 57,2,+2.

### II-c. *The arpeggio six-four chord*

A clear-cut example of an arpeggio six-four chord has not been found. That they actually occurred can scarcely be doubted, especially in the instrumental works where the use of the Basso Continuo does not show this chord in the notation. The following "realization" by Malipiero seems entirely justified by the instrumental procedures of the time.

Freer treatments of the six-four chord by Monteverdi are rare and when they do occur there is usually a question as to the accuracy of the notation or of the translation into modern notation. For example, Malipiero at M. I, 6,2,+2 shows an accented prepared six-four with a skip from the bass.

In a footnote Malipiero gives the following as the original:

But Arnold Mendelssohn[12] gives a solution which, in the light of Monteverdi's usual procedures, seems preferable, and in this interpretation the six-four chord disappears:

H. Leichtentritt,[13] on the other hand, gives an accented six-four chord with a

SIMG. XI, 286.

treatment which does not conform to Monteverdi's usual technique, so that Malipiero's transcription in this case would seem, on internal evidence, to be the more logical.

M. V, 2,1,+1.

---

[12] Monteverdi, *Madrigale*, Neue Folge (ed. Peters; Leipzig), based on the manuscript scores of Dr. Emil Vogel.

[13] *Op. cit.*, p. 286; also in Prunières, H., *op. cit.*

Further, the passage given by Malipiero,

M. XII, 126,1,2.

in which an accented, unprepared six-four occurs with a skip in the bass without the usual resolution, does not seem to be correct, for in the original manuscript[14] the passage stands:

in the next to the top voice, whereby the six-four chord disappears. This version is also given by Haas in DTÖ XXIX, 72,3,2.

Monteverdi's use of the six-four chord may be briefly characterized as follows:

1. The chief types as found in Palestrina continue to appear; the $\left\{\begin{smallmatrix}65-\\4-3\end{smallmatrix}\right.$ formula is the most common.

2. The unprepared six-four again comes into use, but not in prominent or structurally important places.

3. The dissonance is usually prepared in one of the conventional ways; the most important change in the treatment of the dissonance is in the use of freer resolutions.

4. The accented $\begin{smallmatrix}65\\43\end{smallmatrix}$ is frequently used in modulatory passages.

---

[14] "Il ritorno d'Ulisse in patria," MS 18763 (National Bibliotek, Wien), 77,2,+2.

# CHAPTER IX

# THE ENGLISH MADRIGALISTS

### I-A. *The accented (or semi-accented), prepared six-four chord*

THE ACCENTED SIX-FOUR CHORD — $^{65}_{43}$ — in which the fourth is prepared is a fairly common occurrence. Morris[1] says the six-four chord is usually treated as a double suspension; but in view of the many times that the sixth enters freely (i.e., by step or by skip) this statement scarcely seems justified. Except when on the second degree of the scale, it is ordinarily followed by the five-three on the same bass note. Morley used it often on the fifth degree of the scale in a well defined cadence progression, so that there seems little doubt of the appreciation of its cadential qualities either in a full close, some variation of a half-close, or in the deceptive cadence; or if it occurred in the course of a phrase, the $^{65}_{43}$ formula was at times followed by the movement of a third down in the bass to a six-three combination, which may be considered as the first inversion of a tonic chord.

Morley I, 79,3,+2[2]    Morley II, 74,3,4.

Morley IV, 10,2,3.    Morley II, 98,1,2.    Morley II, 19,2,1.

Compare further Morley II, 25,3,1 (B−3 to $^I_6$); II, 100,1,1; 123,2,+1; 124,2,3; III, 82,2,+1 (in phrase); IV, 14,2,+3; 61,1,2; 80,1,+3 (1/2 C); 90,1,1 (B−3 to $^I_6$); 90,2,1 (1/2 C); 94,1,4 (B−1); Orlando Gibbons V, 21,2,3; 36,2,+2; 37,1,+2; 37,1,+1; 48,2,2; 59,1,+1; 64,1,+1 (B−3

---

[1] *Op. cit.*, p. 36.    [2] See Bibliography, under Morley.

to $\frac{1}{6}$); 68,1,3 (B−3 to $\frac{1}{6}$); 68,1,+1 (B−3 to $\frac{1}{6}$); 69,2,3 (with bass skipping a minor sixth across the tenor in the style of an earlier period); 80,2,+2 (in plagal effect $\overset{\text{IV-I}}{6}_4$); 86,2,+2 (deceptive cadence); 91,1,2; 91,2,1; 95,2,1; 99,2,+2 (B+1); 100,1,1/2 (B+1, modulating); 100,1,+1; 101,2,1 (B−3 to five-three); 102,2,2; 113,2,+3 (B−3 to six three); 117,1,+2; 129,1,2; 129,1,+2; 129,2,1; 134,2,1 (deceptive cadence); 135,1,+2; 136,1,+2; 136,2,+2; 137,2,+3 (B−1); 139,2,2; John Wilbye VI, 188,1,+2; Tallis TCM *2*, 4,1,+2;[3] 5,2,+1; Byrd TCM *3*, 2,2,3; 5,1,3; 8,2,12; *4*, 2,1,3; 3,1,+1; *5*, 2,2,1 (1/2 C); 3,1,1 (1/2 C); *25*, 6,1,2; 8,2,2; *28*, 14,2,3; etc.

In a more ornamental form:

Byrd TCM *31*, 9,2,+1.

It would be wrong, however, to assume from the foregoing examples that the English madrigal composers used this combination, i.e., $^{65}_{43}$, exclusively in variations of the cadence formula (where the six-four occurs on the fifth degree of the scale). As with the other composers studied, the accented prepared six-four chord was frequently used near the cadence on other degrees of the scale, particularly on the second, fourth, and sixth degrees, showing that the accented six-four was by no means always the tonic six-four of later terminology. The following example of Byrd, dated *circa* 1589, will serve to illustrate the point. It is also worth studying as an example of music in a transition state from the old modal influence to the modern scalic system. Here vagueness of tonality vies with clear-cut modulation.

Byrd TCM *28*, 11,1,2.

---

[3] For abbreviations see Bibliography, under Tudor Church Music.

The passage begins (speaking in modern terms) in G-major[4]. The following measures may be analyzed in different ways, one of which would be somewhat as follows (mentioning only the six-four chords):

*a*. Six-four on the sixth degree of the scale in G-major

*b*. A tonic six-four in G-major

*c*. Tonic six-four modulating to E-minor followed by a modulation to A-minor

*d*. Tonic six-four in A-minor

*e*. Tonic six-four modulating to G-major (because of *f*-sharp in soprano), followed by a full close in A-minor.

From the modal point of view a more logical explanation is to consider the last portion in the Dorian mode transposed with a six-four chord on the fourth degree before the cadence.

R. O. Morris[5] states that the principle of nearly all the English madrigals is one of key, not of mode. He says further:

The sixteenth-century Modal System, as we saw, was a compromise, in which all the modes tended to lose their identity, and to merge into two general types, clearly foreshadowing our own major and minor scales. The English composers at a comparatively early date seem to have felt that the compromise was doomed, and that a two scale system must replace the old ecclesiastical modes (of which Morley speaks, in the *Plaine and Easie Introduction* of 1597, as something quite antiquated and remote).[6]

But even if the old modal system was in so many respects abandoned it would be inaccurate to maintain that the scalic system followed was strictly that of the modern major and minor, for although old principles were to a large extent outgrown, the new viewpoint was as yet by no means fully attained. It would be more in accordance with the facts to call this a transition period in which are present, side by side, characteristics of both systems. In many compositions occur passages which can obviously be analyzed from the modern major-minor viewpoint as clear-cut modulations etc., but in the same compositions may occur certain elements which are rather to be considered as remnants of the old modal viewpoint, as in the passage from Byrd last quoted.[7]

---

[4] Original, one tone lower.    [5] *Op. cit.*, p. 65.    [6] Morris, *op. cit.*, p. 65.

[7] Whereas from a modern viewpoint the raised sixth degree (*f*-sharp in A-minor) sounds odd in a descending passage, in the Dorian mode it is a perfectly natural procedure.

Transitions of this type are not completed in a day and it is interesting to note how, in the course of the change, factors such as the accented six-four chord, which certainly aided the progress of the new movement, were not infrequently used in such a manner as to indicate that the new viewpoint had not yet entirely displaced the old.

Many analogous examples may be cited in which the six-four chords may be considered as occurring on other degrees of the scale than the fifth; or if it is argued that they are on the fifth degree in a different key and the succeeding passages are modulations, then certainly from a modern viewpoint such abrupt modulations are ill placed or vague.[8] The author is inclined to consider the following example as a transition type of modal procedure with an accented $\overset{65}{\underset{43}{}}$ on the fourth degree—a sort of prototype of a passage in G-minor—rather than to try to give a modulatory significance to the accented six-four chord. Precedent is to be found in Monteverdi (see p. 83), Palestrina (p. 63), Gombert (p. 50), Ockeghem (p. 33), and Dufay (p. 19).

Morley II, 26,2,2.

The procedure may simply be considered as an elaboration of some such simple passage as:

Morley II, 39,2,1.

---

[8] The quotations which are given in the text should not be confused with the type mentioned by Alfred Heuss, *Die Instrumental-Stücke des "Orfeo"* (Inaug. Diss.; Leipzig, 1903), p. 100. Heuss says: ". . . . statt nämlich das zweite Thema so zu richten, dass es nach A-dur gelangt, läuft dasselbe den gleichen Weg wie im ersten Teil; ein Takt vor dem Schluss steht es denn auch in aller Deutlichkeit bereits in D-dur, da sieht der Komponist plötzlich, dass er an einem falschen Ort angelangt ist. Mit Gewalt sucht er einen Weg nach A-dur, was aber missglückt, trotz der Dreingabe eines halben Taktes gegen den ersten Teil."

It is interesting to note that in the means which Heuss characterizes as "mit Gewalt," the accented cadential six-four chord plays a prominent rôle.

in which the third over the third last bass note is delayed by a suspension giving rise to an accented $\frac{65}{43}$ on the fourth degree of the scale without, of course, the usual tonic six-four significance.

Compare the following:

Morley III, 62,1,3.

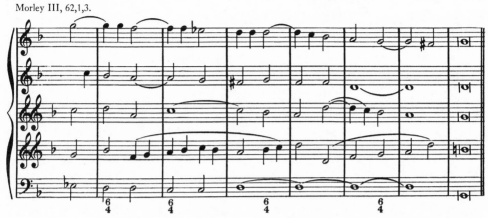

Compare further[9] Morley II, 13,1,2; 26,2,2; 38,1,+1; Morley III, 101,2,2; 107,1,3; IV, 27,1,2; 38,2,3; 74,2,2; Gibbons V, 53,1,+1; 56,2,+2; 69,2,2; 80,1,1; 84,2,1; 127,1,1 $\left(\begin{smallmatrix}6-\\43\end{smallmatrix}\right)$; 141,2,2; 148,1,+1; 148,2,2; Byrd TCM *28*, 4,1,+1; 11,1,2 ff.

The accented (or semi-accented) six-four on the second degree is not uncommon, only here it is usually followed by a six-three on the same bass note.

Morley I, 50,2,1.    Morley IV, 80,1,1.                                    Gibbons V, 23,2,+1.

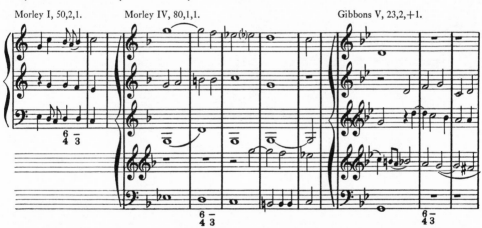

In some instances the sixth is major, in others minor. Compare Gibbons V, 77,2,3/4; 78,2,+2; 89,2,4; 124,2,+2.

When the $\underset{43}{65}$ formula occurs on the second degree, the effect is suggestive of a 15th-century fauxbourdon sort of passage.

---

[9] The tendency for modulatory significance is varied—shading off from clear-cut modulatory passages to those with practically no modulatory implications.

The example, Gibbons V, 53,1,1, also seems to be of the fauxbourdon type—the general movement is in parallel six-three chords with incidental six-fours arising from the use of suspensions etc. At any rate there is no obvious cadential implication in these accented six-four chords.

The $\underset{43}{65}$ on the sixth degree occurs in a number of well defined examples.

See further Gibbons V, 141,2,1; Wilbye VI, 121,1,+1; as well as certain examples referred to below in which the fourth is unprepared.

The following may be regarded as a variation of the six-four on the sixth degree—
the skip from the bass is quite unusual.

Gibbons V, 110,2,1.

I-B. *The accented (or semi-accented), unprepared six-four chord*

The accented six-four chord in which the fourth is not used as a suspension occasionally occurs. The fourth seems to be usually an accented passing note or an appoggiatura, and as such might also be treated with the six-four chords arising from passing or ornamental notes. The examples noted show the six-four on the sixth degree with relation to the cadence.

Morley I, 101,2,+2.                          Morley I, 102,2,1.

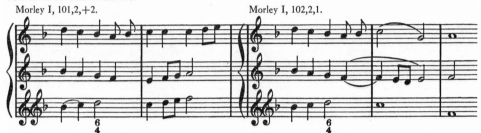

Morris[10] cites two examples from Tye, where the fourth is approached by skip on the accent, and in one of them it is accompanied by a sixth.

Tye, Missa, "Euge bone,"
Morris, *op. cit.*, Ex. p. 44.

II-A. *The auxiliary six-four chord*

The chords of this category may be divided into two main groups, as in Monteverdi,
(1) $\left\{ \begin{smallmatrix} 65 \\ 43 \end{smallmatrix} \right.$ and (2) $\left\{ \begin{smallmatrix} 65- \\ 4-3 \end{smallmatrix} \right|$.

1. The auxiliary $\begin{smallmatrix} 65 \\ 43 \end{smallmatrix}$ occurs so regularly on the fifth or the first degree of the scale that it seems quite natural to consider all such combinations as being so placed; therefore, when it occurs on other degrees of the scale, it is simply understood as having this relation in another key—hence as producing modulation.

[10] *Op. cit.*, Ex. p. 44.

It will be noticed that the fourth as well as the sixth is approached by step or by skip; that it usually resolves downward by step; that the combination most frequently occurs on the unaccented portion of the bar, but occasionally also on the stronger accent; that the $\left\{ {}^{65-}_{4-3} \right.$ combination is usually preferred for the last combination before the final in a cadence.

The following examples may be cited to give some idea of the frequency of this combination:

Morley I, 10,3,3; 15,3,2; 32,2,+1; 44,2,+1; 45,3,+2/1; 48,2,+2/1; 63,2,+1; 77,3,2; 86,3,3; 89,3,+3; 93,3,3; 96,3,4/5; 102,3,+2; 103,1,3; II, 8,2,2; 9,2,+1; 14,2,+2; 33,2,+1; 33,3,1/2/3 (seven examples in four measures—a pedal effect ending with the usual $\left\{ {}^{65-}_{4-3} \right. \mid$ cadence); 44,3,1/2 (there seems to be an error in notation—the two middle parts should obviously come a half note earlier in which case the cadence formula falls into the familiar $\left\{ {}^{65-}_{4-3} \right.$ position); 67,2,+1 (two examples); 67,3,1 (two examples); 67,3,2 (two examples); 67,3,3 (two examples); 70,2,1; 72,3,3; 77,3,1; 87,2,1; 100,1,2; 100,3,2; 106,1,2; III, 4,1,+3; 22,2,2; 23,2,3; 32,2,1; 37,2,3; 40,2,2; 71,2,1.

Examples in which the six-four serves as the resolution of the $\overset{V}{7}$ emphasize the chordal nature (i.e., as an inversion of the tonic chord) of the six-four combination.

Morley III, 71,2,1.

134,2,2; 141,2,3; IV, 59,1,1/2 (four examples); 61,1,1; 75,1,+1; 75,2,3; 78,1,3; 82,2,2; 83,2,2 (two examples); O. Gibbons V, 13,1,+2 $\left( {}^{\#\ 6-}_{43} \left| {}^{6}_{3} \right. \right)$; 34,1,+1; 34,2,1; 35,1,1/2; 37,2,+2/1;

40,1,3/4; 57,2,3/4; 58,2,1/2/3; 61,1,+1; 80,1,+2; 97,1,+2; 97,2,1; 98,1,2; 98,1,+2; 119,1,+1; 125,1,1; 125,1,+1; 145,1,+2.

Certain procedures such as Morley IV, 89,1,+3,

Morley IV, 89,1,+3.

are reminiscent of the Dufay period.

2. The $\begin{Bmatrix} 65- \\ 4-3 \end{Bmatrix}$ is, with the English madrigal composers as with their Italian contemporaries, by far the most common relation in which the six-four chord occurs. The following may serve as master examples:

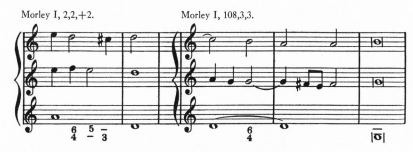

Morley I, 2,2,+2.      Morley I, 108,3,3.

The following citations show many variations but belong to the same classification, and will give an idea of the frequency of the device:

Morley I, 5,2,4; 6,3,3; 7,1,1; 8,1,2; 9,2,+1; 10,1,3; 10,3,2; 12,1,3; 20,3,+3; 26,3,+3; 28,3,4; 29,3,2; etc.,—45 other examples in this volume.

Morley II, 2,2,+2; 6,3,+2; 8,3,1; 9,3,+3; 11,2,1; 11,3,+3; 12,1,+2; 12,3,+1; 14,2,1; 14,3,1; 15,1,+3; 18,2,+2; etc.,—80 other examples in this volume.

Morley III, 4,1,+2; 11,2,3; 14,1,3; 16,2,2; 17,2,2; 19,2,+2; 21,2,+2; 22,2,+2; 23,2,4; 24,2,+2; 25,2,+2; 28,2,3; etc.,—58 other examples in this volume.

Morley IV, 2,1,+1; 7,2,3; 12,2,+3; 14,1,2; 15,2,+2; 16,2,2; 18,2,3; 20,2,+2; 22,2,2; 24,1,+2; 27,1,3; 30,1,1; 35,1,+1; etc.,—38 other examples in this volume.

Gibbons V, 2,2,1; 2,2,+1; 3,1,+1; 3,2,+2; 5,2,+2; 7,1,1; 8,1,+1; 10,2,2; 17,1,+2; 18,1,1; 24,1,2; 24,2,1; 27,2,2; etc.,—84 other examples in this volume.

Wilbye, VI, 1,2,1; 3,1,+1; 5,2,3; 8,1,1; 8,2,+2; 9,1,+2; 9,3,+3; etc.; Wm. Byrd TCM *3*, 2,1,+2; *4*, 4,1,+2; *5*, 3,2,2; 6,1,2; etc.; Weelkes TCM *17*, 4,1,+2; 9,1,1; 11,1,+2; etc.

A few variations whose relation to the $\begin{Bmatrix} 65- \\ 4-3 \end{Bmatrix}$ will be obvious may be cited. There are of course many others.

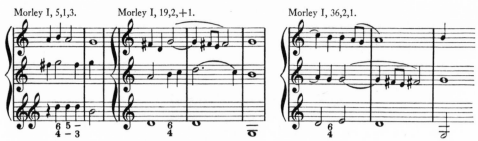

Another formula which frequently occurs is:

Here the six-four is replaced by what moderns would call the tonic chord in root posi-tion. This is cited as another of the possible ways in which the idea of tonic quality may have been carried over to the six-four chord used in the same relative position.

## II-B. *The passing six-four chord*

The unaccented six-four resulting from the use of passing and other ornamental notes occurs in the works of the English madrigal composers as in those of the other composers studied. A few examples which may be considered as typical are cited. Further comment seems unnecessary.

----

[11] See further Morley I, 16,2,+1; 17,3,1; 28,1,1; 49,3,1; etc.

Compare further Morley I, 35,1,1; 81,1,2; 90,1,2; 110,3,1; Morley II, 52,2,2; 46,2,1; 72,2, +3; 72,3,2; Morley III, 11,1,2; Gibbons V, 57,2,2; 92,2,+2.

The following example, in which the bass of the six-four is treated as a suspension, is unusual but none the less interesting, especially in view of the fact that a similar idiom has been found in the works of other composers.[12]

Theoretically it might properly be classed as a variation of the accented, prepared six-four. But if one remembers that bar lines do not exist in the original editions[13] and that the accentuation is often irregular, one can readily see the close affinity, in certain contexts, between the "accented, prepared" and the "passing" six-four.

---

[12] See Monteverdi VI, 10,2,+2, cited p. 93 of the present work; compare Gom. T. M. 1844 R, 21,1,2, cited p. 56; and Ockeghem 57,2,3, p. 38.

[13] See Fellowes in the Preface to Morley I; p. iv.

In Gibbons V, 123,2,2, the six-four chord is approached in a somewhat similar manner, but its further treatment is more like a variation of the $\left\{\begin{smallmatrix} 65- \\ 4-3 \end{smallmatrix}\right.$ formula.

Gibbons V, 123,2,2.

## II-c. *The arpeggio six-four chord*

As has been observed in the other vocal music so far examined, the arpeggio six-four does not occur in any clear-cut fashion. The following shows the fourth in this relation but the sixth does not accompany it. It suggests, however, the possibility of such an occurrence.

Morley I, 33,1,1.

In general, the English madrigal composers treated the six-four chord very much as did their Italian contemporaries. Although the accented unprepared six-four was used to some extent, most of the six-four chords were prepared and resolved in the conventional ways; the free resolutions of the Monteverdi type were seldom used. The constant use of these chords in cadence formulae, often effecting modulation, was doubtless significant for the whole future evolution of music, because it was out of just such situations that a new conception of tonality as well as the modern major and minor scalic system developed.

# CHAPTER X

## THE INSTRUMENTAL MUSIC

THAT THE CONSCIOUSNESS of the six-four chord as the inversion of a triad was furthered by instrumental procedures is scarcely to be doubted. The fanfare passages on wind instruments (horns or trumpets especially) must surely have produced this effect. For example, if three wind instruments, such as trumpets or horns of the same pitch, were played together, the available notes being those of the overtone series, 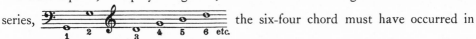 the six-four chord must have occurred in some such form as 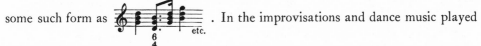 . In the improvisations and dance music played on the various other instruments, similar combinations must also have occurred. The difficulties facing the investigator who wants to find direct evidence of such practice in noted music are well known. They arise, of course, because of the comparatively late development of an accurate notation for instrumental music.[1] Not until the beginning of the 16th century do independent instrumental compositions appear in a notation which is reasonably dependable and accurate. That a long, preliminary period of development preceded this century is obvious, but for present purposes the investigation can scarcely be carried beyond the 16th century except in a conjectural way.

The dependence of much of the instrumental music on vocal procedures is equally well known[2] and it is to be expected that in the use of the six-four chord comparatively few if any fundamentally different treatments will be found. Only in the arpeggio type of six-four is a form discovered which must be considered as distinctly arising from the nature of instrumental technique. An investigation of the available instrumental music shows the above assumptions to be essentially correct. The various types of six-four chords already traced in vocal music are to be found in the instrumental music as well.

### I-A. *The accented (or semi-accented), prepared six-four chord*

A passage from Juan Bermudo shows this chord in a conventional relation to the final.

Juan Bermudo (Kinkeldey)[3], 228,6,2.

---

[1] See Adler-Fischer, pp. 382 ff.     [2] *Ibid.*, p. 383.

[3] Kinkeldey, O., *Orgel und Klavier in der Musik des 16. Jahrhunderts* (Leipzig, 1910).

In the next citations from J. Buus, a certain cadential impression is created either by the skip of the fifth in the bass or by a plagal treatment.

J. Buus[4] (Wasielewski), 35,4,+2.    *Ibid.*, 37,1,+2.                                        *Ibid.*, 40,3,3.

The following examples illustrate the use of the accented (or semi-accented) six-four chord (with fourth prepared) in situations having a more or less clearly defined conventional relation to the cadence formula in its different aspects.

Hans v. Constanz,          Ammerbach tabulatur,          Schlick, Jr.[5]
VjfMW V, 153,3,2.          VjfMW V, 79,1,1.              VjfMW V, 78,1,2.

\* (Fourth "prepared" in the octave.)

G. Cavazzoni[6] (Torchi) III, 4,3,2.          *Ibid.*, 7,3,+2.

[4] Wasielewski, J., *Geschichte der Instrumentalmusik im XVI. Jahrhundert* (Berlin, 1878).
[5] Quoted by Carl Paesler, "Fundamentalbuch von Hans v. Constanz," VjfMW, 5: 78.
[6] Torchi, L., *L'Arte Musicale in Italia* (Milan), vol. 3.

Compare further the following examples from Torchi III: Cavazzoni (1542), 5,1,1; 5,2,1; 6,2,2; 12,5,1; 13,4,+2; 13,5,2; 13,6,+2; 17,2.+2; 28,1,2; 41,5,1; Valenti (1580), 47,2,1; 48,3,2; Bertoldo (1591), 59,3,+2; 60,3,+2; 60,5,+2; A. Gabrieli (1595), 61,5,1; 63,4,2; 65,2,2; 65,5,1; 65,6,+1; 68,4,1; Padovano (1604), 80,4,1; Merulo (1604), 95,1,1; 101,2,1; 102,2,1; 102,2,2; 103,1,1; 103,4,1; 104,4,1; 117,4,+1; 123,3,1; 130,6,1; G. Paolo Cima (1609), 142,1,1; 143,1,1; Ascanio Majone (1609), 149,4,3; 150,3,1; C. Antegnati (1608), 156,2,+2; 156,4,+1; 157,6,+1; 159,1,1; 159,2,+1; 159,5,1; G. Fatorini (1622), 161,5,+2.

However, the $\underset{43}{65}$ formula in the instrumental music, as was seen to be true in the vocal music, was not exclusively used on the fifth or first degree of the scale but also on the sixth or second degree (less often on the fourth and other degrees of the scale), although in decreasing frequency as the feeling for modern scalic relations grew.

---

[7] Showing movement in the bass while the fourth resolves—obviously a variation of usual procedures. The following example from A. Gabrieli (Torchi) III, 70,2,4, probably belongs in the same category:

A. Gabrieli (Torchi) III, 70,2,+1.

Some typical examples may be cited:

⁸ *Ricercari per organo.*

Hans v. Constanz, VjfMW V, 150,4,2.[9]                    Attaingnant (Kinkeldey), 261,6,2.

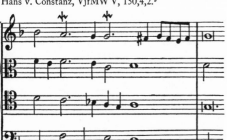

Compare further Cavazzoni (Torchi) III, 2,2,2; 8,2,2; 17,4,+2; 19,1,1.

The $^{65}_{43}$ on the sixth degree before the cadence may be considered simply as an ornamentation of such an example as the following and as having only a slight "cadential six-four" feeling in the usual sense.

Hans v. Constanz, VjfMW, 158,3,+2.

The fact that the cadential six-four was so commonly used in the modern sense probably accounts for the short duration of the six-four itself in the majority of examples cited. On the other hand, there is a manifest tendency, particularly with the English madrigal composers, to let the usual cadential effect find its natural play, in which case a modulation of shorter or longer duration takes place. In other words,[10] the use of the six-four chord on other degrees of the scale than one and five has a tendency to make these other degrees felt as a one or five in a new tonal relation; hence it helps to promote modulation and the intentional playing of one key against another for the purpose of contrast.

The six-four chord with the bass treated as a suspension discord occurs occasionally.

Cavazzoni (Torchi) III, 8,1,+1.          Padovano (Torchi) III, 88,3,2.

[9] As if on the fourth degree of the scale. Compare with the Padovano 87,3,1, cited above.
[10] See also the preceding chapter.

At times, just as in some of the vocal music already examined, the fourth seems to resolve up by step in the bass.

A. Gabrieli (Torchi) III, 66,3,+2.

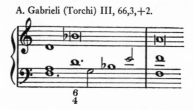

### I-B. *The accented (or semi-accented), unprepared six-four chord*

That the unprepared six-four should occur in the instrumental as in the vocal music of the various periods is only to be expected. The appearance of this combination, however, is relatively infrequent. An example may be cited from Conrad Paumann's *Fundamentum organisandi* (1452)[11] which occurs under the name W. Legrant.[12]

W. Legrant (Chrysander Jahrbuch) II, 204,1,2.

Here the fourth is approached and quitted conjunctly, the resolution to the five-three being quite according to rule. The cadential relation is more difficult to determine. The rest of the compositions in the *Orgelbuch* are mostly for two voices—in the passages in three parts no accented six-four combination has been found.

Paesler[13] cites an unprepared six-four from Schlick, Jr. (*De signis musicalibus*), whom he names as the first to permit such uses to appear in the examples introduced in his theoretical writings.

Schlick, Jr., VjfMW V, 78,2,2.

Buchner (Hans v. Constanz),[14] the first, according to Paesler,[15] to discuss the six-four combination specifically and to mention its free approach as allowable, used it in this way very sparingly. Paesler also cites the following example:

---

[11] Transcribed from the Tabulatur by F. W. Arnold, revised by H. Bellermann; Chrysander Jahrbuch 2 (1867), No. 28.

[12] A question is raised whether this composition was in the original Organ-book or was added later. See Adler-Fischer, p. 385.

[13] *Op. cit.*, p. 78.

[14] *Fundamentalbuch* (1551), ed. by Paesler, *q. v.*

[15] *Op. cit.*, p. 76.

Buchner (Hans v. Constanz), VjfMW V, 78,3,+1.    *Ibid.*, VjfMW V, 78,4,3.

A further examination of the *Fundamentalbuch* reveals only the following further example, which is also given by Paesler with question marks (presumably as to the rectitude of the transcription).

Hans v. Constanz, VjfMW V, 187,2,+1.

Paesler[16] considers that Ammerbach made the final step in the free use of the six-four chord. ". . . . Bei ihm ist dieser Akkord nicht nur in Kadenzen etwas ganz Gewöhnliches und fast Unvermeidliches oder Notwendiges, sondern auch im freien Einsatz wird er öfters gebraucht." Only one example is given to support this statement:

Ammerbach, VjfMW V, 79,1,+1.

As in vocal music, the accented, unprepared six-four usually arises from the use of accented passing notes or other ornamental devices. The following examples may be given.

Cavazzoni (Torchi) III,6,3,2    Bertoldo (Torchi) III, 59,4,1.    Padovano (Torchi) III, 79,4,1.

---

[16] *Op. cit.*, p. 77.

### II-A. *The auxiliary six-four chord*

The auxiliary six-four in instrumental music has little novelty. The same basic procedures of vocal music are followed, oftentimes being more ornamental in the treatment of the melodic line. For example, the typical six-four of Dufay following the seven-four suspension on the second degree in a cadence, is found in Paumann's *Orgelbuch* in a composition (No. 26) under the name of Puteheim.[17]

Paumanns Orgelbuch (Chrysander Jahrbuch) II, 217,4,1.

Variations of this are common in the *Fundamentalbuch* of Hans von Constanz.

Hans v. Constanz, VjfMW V, 114,3,+1.

Compare further Hans von Constanz, VjfMW V, 121,2,1; 138,2,1; 143,2,+1; 152,1,2; etc.

A clear example of the auxiliary six-four from the first half of the 16th century is shown in Cavazzoni (Torchi) III, 5,5,+2.[18] A number of examples of variations of this type of six-four may be found in Hans von Constanz.

Hans v. Constanz, VjfMW V, 100,1,1.

Schlick tabulatur (1512), VjfMW V, 77,2,+1.

See further Hans von Constanz, *op. cit.*, 123,2,1/2/3; 124,1,+1; 127,1,2; 127,4,+1; 137,5,2; 164,4,1; 164,4,+1; 164,5,2; 69,1,+2.

---

[17] Arnold, W. F., Chrysander Jahrbuch, 2 (1867): 217,4,1. The middle part is incomplete as given, but the analogy is obvious.

[18] See p. 113.

The auxiliary $\left\{\begin{smallmatrix}65-\\4-3\end{smallmatrix}\right.$ occurs in various ornamental forms in instrumental music.

Schlick tabulatur (1512), VjfMW V, 77,1,1.

Kotter tabulatur, VjfMW V, 77,3,2.

Hans v. Constanz, VjfMW V, 155,4,1.          Cavazzoni (Torchi) III, 13,5,+2.

Hans v. Constanz, VjfMW V, 125,3,2.

Compare further the following examples from Torchi III: Cavazzoni (1542), 34,3,1; Pellegrini (1599), 49,4,2; 49,5,1; 51,6,1; Bertoldo (1591), 56,6,+1; A. Gabrieli (1595), 62,5,+2; 65,1,1; 65,1,+1; 72,3,+2; 77,2,1; C. Merulo (1604), 93,5,1; 96,5,+1; 96,6,1; 100,2,2; 108,1,1; 114,1,1; 130,1,1; Paolo Cima (1606), 142,1,+1; Ascanio Majone (1609), 146,3,+1; L. Luzzaschi (1622/25), 150,6,+2; 151,1,2; Fatorini (1622), 162,2,1; etc.

An interesting example, which contains all the foregoing types of six-four chords as well as several which the author classes under "passing" six-fours, occurs in one of the organ works of M. Praetorius.[19] The composition is 59 measures in length and has no less than 27 six-four chords. These may be classified as follows:

| | | |
|---|---|---|
| Accented prepared | $\left(\begin{smallmatrix} 6 & 5 \\ 4 & 3 \end{smallmatrix}\right)$ | 5 |
| Accented unprepared | $\left(\begin{smallmatrix} 6 & 5 \\ 4 & 3 \end{smallmatrix}\right)$ | 1 |
| Auxiliary | $\left(\begin{smallmatrix} 6 & 5 \\ 4 & 3 \end{smallmatrix}\right)$ | 14 |
| Auxiliary | $\left(\begin{smallmatrix} 6 & 5 & - \\ 4 & - & 3 \end{smallmatrix}\right)$ | 4 |
| Passing | $\left(\begin{smallmatrix} 6 \\ 4 \end{smallmatrix}\right)$ | 3 |
| | Total | 27 |

The composition is well worth studying as a whole. The following excerpts are cited here—the beginning, two passages from the middle portion, and the last few bars.

M. Praetorius, AfMW III, 137,1,1.

Ibid., 137,2,+1.

Ibid., 137,4,1.

[19] "A Solis ortus, etc." (*Hymnodia Sionia* [Wolfenbüttel, 1611] No. 26), "Pro Organo a 5," in AfMW, 3: 137 f.

*Ibid.*, 138,5,2.

The mixture of modal and modern major-minor procedures is clearly illustrated. The beginning suggests the Dorian mode (not D-minor because of the *b*-naturals) until the fifth bar where the *b*-flat and the ensuing cadence with the $\left.\begin{matrix}657\\43-\end{matrix}\right\}$ formula produces a strong D-minor close followed by a deceptive cadence in A-minor. The next $_{43}^{65}$ has the effect of a plagal six-four in C-major (137,3,1). The $_{4}^{6}$ at 137,3,5 (*a* in bass) could be classed as a $_{4}^{6}$ on the sixth degree in C-major followed by the only unprepared accented six-four in the composition, which together with the following bars (137,4,1 ff.) gives a clear-cut passage in C-major, although the full close is avoided as inappropriate in the course of a composition.

The final bars (138,5,2 ff.) are obviously modal in treatment (modified phrygian cadence). They need no further comment here, but are most interesting to study!

The six-four chords in the following works of Praetorius[20] show a similar distribution among the various types, the favorite, that is, the one appearing most frequently, being the auxiliary $_{43}^{65}$. In No. 3, "Summo parenti gloria" etc., *pro Organo a 4*, which begins on *d* and ends on *e*, six-four chords occur on *e, f, g, a, b,* and *c*—every degree of the mode except *d*, some accented-prepared, some auxiliary, some in clear-cut modulatory combinations (often with plagal effects), and occasionally as mere passing combinations.

### II-B. *The passing six-four chord*

A few examples of passing six-four chords and those arising from other decorative notes may be cited.

Hans v. Constanz,
VjfMW V, 100,2,1.          *Ibid.*, 115,2,1.

---

[20] AfMW, 3: 139 ff.

Compare *ibid.*, 117,1,+1; 117,3,+1; 161,2,2; 164,1,+1.

### II-c. *The arpeggio six-four chord*

The arpeggio six-four chord is the distinct contribution of instrumental music to the development of the concept of the six-four chord as a triad inversion. The following example from Merulo will illustrate the type.

Merulo (Torchi) III, 105,4,1.

---

[21] This example may also be considered as a variation of the treatment of an accented-prepared $\frac{6}{4}$. Because, however, of the lack of cadential effect and the flowing character of the bass, the author prefers to consider it rather as a passing effect.

The possibility of the occurrence of such combinations in all situations in which arpeggio-like figures are possible—on wind instruments of the same pitch overblowing on the notes of the natural harmonies, and on harp-like instruments, etc.—has already been mentioned. Clear-cut examples in musical notation are difficult to find before the 16th century. Two obvious reasons may be mentioned. It was not until this comparatively late period that the keyboard instruments were developed sufficiently—notably the organ—to make possible the playing of chords with the right hand, while the left hand played florid passages (or vice versa). The early organ, as is well known, was so constructed that only melodies could be played—the keys being struck with the fist (or with the foot). Even in Paumann the music is chiefly for two voices. In the first half of the 16th century, in the works of Schlick, Kleber, Kotter, Buchner (Hans von Constanz), etc., together with more or less similar developments in France, Italy, England, and other countries, great progress is shown so that by the second half of the 16th century and the beginning of the 17th century, examples of such procedures may be found in abundance. The second reason making it difficult to trace the arpeggio six-four chord is the late development of the notation of instrumental music.

If the style of the instrumental music follows vocal procedures, the arpeggio six-four chord does not appear any oftener than the corresponding vocal types; but where the more characteristic instrumental devices appear, the arpeggio six-four chord is very likely to show itself. It is characteristic of this style that the fifth of the triad appears in the bass with free treatment, such as the approach and (or) quitting by skip, in such a way that there can be no question that it is an essential note of the harmony. In the following example from A. Gabrieli, the two *e*'s in the bass, obviously essential notes in the chord, give rise to six-four chords not only unaccented but also at least "semi-unaccented." Although the second *e* occurs in a scale passage, the fact that it is a member of the chord in the right hand precludes its being considered as a passing note in the usual sense of the term.

A. Gabrieli (Torchi) III, 78,6,1.

Many variations occur of which only a few are cited.

Cavazzoni (Torchi) III, 9,4,1.        Pellegrini (Torchi) III, 54,2,+1.

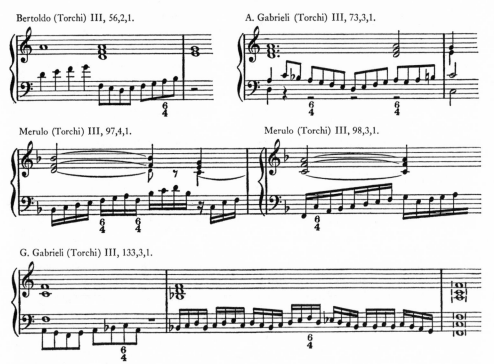

Bertoldo (Torchi) III, 56,2,1.          A. Gabrieli (Torchi) III, 73,3,1.

Merulo (Torchi) III, 97,4,1.          Merulo (Torchi) III, 98,3,1.

G. Gabrieli (Torchi) III, 133,3,1.

Many similar examples may be cited from Torchi III: Pellegrini (1599), 54,5,1; A. Gabrieli (1596), 70,3,1/2; 70,4,1; 73,3,1; 73,4,1; 74,1,1/2; 75,3,2; 76,4,+1; 76,5,1/2; 76,5,+1; 76,6,+1; 77,3,1/2; etc., etc.; Merulo (1604), 96,3,1; 97,1,1; 97,2,1; 97,3,1; 97,4,1; 98,3,1; 98,4,1; 99,4,1; 103,3,1; 105,2,1; 105,4,1; etc., etc.; G. Gabrieli (1593), 133,3,1; 133,5,2; 133,6,1/2; 135,5,1; 136,2,2; 137,1,2; 138,1,2; 138,2,1/2; etc., etc.; L. Luzzaschi, 152,2,5; 152,3,1; 152,5,1; C. Antegnati (1608), 155,4,+1; 155,6,+2; 159,2,2; G. Diruta (1625), 165,3,1; 165,4,2; 165,5,1/2; 166,1,1; 166,4,1; 166,5,2/3; etc., etc.

Such a free treatment of the six-four chord as the following must be considered as the outcome of the growing consciousness of the six-four position of a triad as a possible, nearly independent, tonal entity.

A. Gabrieli (Torchi) III, 72,4,2.

These and countless other examples show that the six-four chord in all its essential forms was clearly developed in musical practice before the middle of the 17th century. In fact, examples of every type of six-four chord have been found in music published before the death of Palestrina! As the next chapter indicates, not until later did the theorists come to classify this combination as the inversion of a triad.

# CHAPTER XI

## THE THEORISTS

IT IS TRUE that the music theorists of antiquity seemed to account for the common intervals of European music. But modern researchers are of the opinion that their only uses of these intervals were in the establishment of a scalic system and in their practical application on that basis in the development of melodies, and that they had no knowledge of music in more than one part either in the form of independent voices moving along together or in the shape of a melody in an upper voice accompanied by chords in a functional relation. Thus a concept of counterpoint, harmony, and chord in the modern sense was entirely foreign to them.[1]

The 9th century A.D. is usually given as the time when in the history of European music the definite beginnings of music in more than one part are to be found.[2] The treatise "Musica Enchiriadis" attributed to Hucbald of St. Amand in the second half of the 9th (or beginning of the 10th) century, describes a system of singing known as "Organum."[3] Up to then, the term "interval" was used in a melodic sense (successive occurrence in a melody), but from that time on, it is also used in a harmonic sense (simultaneous occurrence in a chordal combination).

The three most important constituent intervals of the ancient [Greek] system, octave, fifth, and fourth, which formed the limits of the scales and tetrachords and at the same time the intervals with the simplest mathematical relations as already determined on the monochord by Pythagoras, i.e., 1:2, 2:3, 3:4, show themselves now as the three most important constituent intervals in the new system.[4]

Besides the singing in parallel octaves, which occurs naturally when men and women (or boys with unchanged voices) sing together (hence not a new invention), one finds also the singing in parallel fifths and fourths (with doubling in the octave) as a conscious contribution in the writings of this period. That such a procedure must have been common in music practice long before is evidenced by the often observed fact that when a large group of people are singing (or whistling) together, the fourth and fifth can usually be quite distinctly heard.

The simple Organum in the fourth according to Hucbald[5] is:

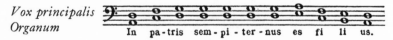

*Vox principalis*
*Organum*

In  pa - tris  sem - pi - ter - nus  es  fi  li  us.

---

[1] Adler-Abert-Sachs, p. 39; compare further Coussemaker, C. E. H. de, *L'Art Harmonique* (Paris, 1865), p. 35; *Histoire de l'Harmonie au Moyen-âge* (Paris, 1852), pp. 3 ff.

[2] Apart from some suggestion of heterophonic music in the time of the Greeks (Adler-Abert-Sachs, p. 56 and Adler-Ludwig, p. 159) and among primitive peoples (see Adler-Lach, pp. 8 ff.). Compare Coussemaker, *L'Art Harmonique*, pp. 36 ff.; Coussemaker, *Hist. de l'Harmonie au Moyen-âge*, pp. 3 ff. and Riemann, *Geschichte der Musiktheorie*, (Leipzig, 1898), pp. 17 ff.

[3] Adler-Ludwig, pp. 118 and 163; for a fuller discussion see: Riemann, *Geschichte der Musiktheorie*, pp. 17 ff.; MacPherson, *A Short History of Harmony* (London), pp. 21 ff.; Shirlaw, *The Theory of Harmony* (London, 1917), p. 1; *Oxford History of Music* (Oxford Univ. Press, 1905), 2, pp. 1 ff.; Coussemaker, *L'Art Harmonique* (1865) pp. 36 ff.; *Hist. de l'Harmonie au Moyen-âge* (1852), pp. 12 ff.; Hucbald *in* Gerbert, *Scriptores Ecclesiastici de Musica* (1784), pp. 104 ff., 152 ff.

[4] Adler-Ludwig, p. 163; compare further Hucbald *in* Gerbert, *op. cit.*: 160, "Symphoniae simplices ac primae sunt tres quibus reliquae componuntur ex quibus una est, quam diatessaron vocant, altera diapente, tertia diapason."

[5] "Musica Enchiriadis," Gerbert *Script.*, 1: 165 (transcription into modern notation according to Riemann, *op. cit.*, p. 29); for examples of the other types of Organum see Riemann, *op. cit.*, p. 80; Coussemaker, *Hist. de l'Harmonie au Moyen-âge*, p. 15, and Gerbert *Script.*, p. 188.

The next example[6] shows the abandonment of the pure parallel fourth progressions, in which however the fourth still plays a prominent part:

The significance of such a change for the development of independent part writing is well known.[7] Examples from actual musical practice are few, but by the beginning of the 13th century the essential steps in the development of so-called melodic and rhythmic independence had been made and the great polyphonic period which had its culmination in the work of Palestrina, was ushered in.

Guido of Arezzo (+1050)[8] is the first theorist after Hucbald to give a detailed account of the Organum. The fourth as the interval on which the parallel progression of the voices primarily rested, is emphasized.[9] In the course of the 11th century, however, the preference for the fourth seems to have been given up,[10] and in the Discantus of the 12th century only the octave (or unison) and the fifth were permissible consonants.[11] The significance of this, of course, is that the fourth as well as the other intervals could occur as passing notes between octaves and fifths (Riemann, *op. cit.*, p. 108):

At the same time greater importance seems gradually to have been placed on the third and sixth. The movement in this direction may very possibly have had its beginnings in the 10th and 11th centuries in northern Europe (northern England, Denmark, and other lands).[12] Just who was the first to teach that the thirds were consonant

---

[6] Adler-Ludwig, p. 165.

[7] See Adler-Ludwig, p. 166 for example.

[8] Riemann, *op. cit.*, p. 73; Coussemaker, *Hist. de l'Harmonie au Moyen-âge*, p. 25.

[9] Jeppesen's statement, *op. cit.*, p. 86, ". . . . In the earliest Organum, though, there is a preference for fourths above all other intervals, while later,—for instance in Guido of Arezzo's 'Micrologus,' dating from the 11th century— fifths predominate," seems to be directly opposed to Riemann's view. Guido in cap. 18 of the "Micrologus" (Gerbert *Script.*, 2: 21, quoted by Riemann, *op. cit.*, p. 73) expressly designates the fourth (. . . . ut canenti semper chorda quarta succedat ut A et D, ubi si organum per acutum a duplices, ut sit D a, resonabit A ad D diatessaron . . . .) as the interval of the added voice below the cantus, and confirms it with the example:

$$\text{Diapente} \begin{cases} & c \ d \ e \\ \text{Diatessaron} & \begin{cases} F \ G \ a \\ C \ D \ E \end{cases} \end{cases} \text{etc.}$$

and in the following passage states that his system does not admit the fifth (or the minor second). Riemann interprets it so and says (*op. cit.*, p. 82) "Die Quinte lehnt Guido für das Organum rundweg ab. . . . ."

Compare Amb. II: 163: ". . . . lehrt Guido ein Organum, in lauter Quarten . . . . etc." Also Adler-Ludwig, p. 165: "Guido lehnt z. B., die Quint für die von ihm bevorzugte Organumart völlig ab!" Regarding G. Jacobsthal, *Die chromatische Alteration*, etc., p. 271, Riemann says (p. 81) Jacobsthal ". . . . hat nicht scharf genug gesehen, als er die Quinte für das wichtigste Intervall im Organum erklärte und das Quartenorganum sozusagen als eine allerlei Konzessionen erfordernde Abart des eigentlichen Organums hinstellte . . . ."

That the fifth in Guido's time may have been preferred by many is very likely. For example John Cotton, *ca.* 1100, (Gerbert 2: 230 ff.; Riemann, *op. cit.*, p. 92; Adler-Ludwig, *op. cit.*, p. 165) gives one to understand that different people thought (or did) differently with respect to the diaphony ("Ea diversi diverse utuntur").

[10] Riemann, *op. cit.*, p. 92; Riemann's conclusion is based on the testimony of John Cotton (Gerbert, 2: 230 ff.).

[11] *Ibid.*, pp. 97 ff. The fourth is mentioned in this connection in the writings of Gui de Châlis (Coussemaker, *Hist. de l'Harmonie au Moyen-âge*, pp. 255 ff., and *Script.*, 2: 191 ff.; see Riemann, *op. cit.*, pp. 104 f.

[12] See Adler-Ludwig, *op. cit.*, p. 166; Riemann, *op. cit.*, pp. 111 ff. and especially the brief but excellent discussion of this point by Jeppesen, *op. cit.*, pp. 86 ff.

(although imperfect) is difficult to determine.[13] It will suffice here to point out that in the 13th century Johannes de Garlandia[14] divides the intervals into:

I. Consonant:
- (a) Perfect.............................unison and octave
- (b) Intermediate.....................fifth and fourth
- (c) Imperfect.........................major and minor third

II. Dissonant:
- (a) Perfect.............................minor second, augmented fourth, and major seventh
- (b) Intermediate.....................major second and minor sixth
- (c) Imperfect.........................major sixth and minor seventh

Here the fourth is classed as an intermediate consonance (the augmented as a perfect dissonance), while the minor sixth is classed as an intermediate dissonance and the major sixth as imperfect.

Franco (of Paris?)[15] follows primarily the same classification except that he divides the dissonances into two classes, perfect and imperfect, putting the minor sixth with the perfect dissonances and the major second with the imperfect.

The *Compendium discantus*[16] gives a still different classification including the minor sixth with the pure dissonances and the major sixth "in a progression to the octave"[17] with the consonances (*per accidens*). The statement regarding the fourth is "Consonantiarum . . . .; una est perfecta, et non per accidens," which Riemann takes to mean "Eine ist an sich *konsonant*, wird aber durch den Zusammenhang zur *Dissonanz*." Shirlaw says, "The perfect Fourth, although in itself *consonant*, has the effect of a *dissonance*." But these conclusions read more into the passage than is actually there because the sentence in question is not speaking of *dissonances* at all but of *consonances*, so that the passage should properly be interpreted, "One [of the *consonances*] is perfect or imperfect (not-perfect) according to the context in which it occurs."

Jeppesen seems to corroborate this point of view[18] in that he counts the fourth among the consonants in his researches in this period.

Also, Marchettus of Padua, in his *Lucidarium musicae planae*[19] (1274), still includes the fourth with the consonances while he places the third and sixth under the heading of "bearable" or "tolerable" dissonances or diaphonia. These are "tolerable" dissonances in the sense that in each case both tones, by a simultaneous movement, one up and the other down, arrive at a consonance, whereas in the other dissonances such a relation is not possible.

It is obvious that in the period from the 10th to the 13th century the ideas of consonance and dissonance, and their treatment, were gradually becoming clarified in the musical world. Many problems are still unsolved, but a beginning has definitely been made. Jeppesen[20] considers the Franconian law, propounded about the middle of the 13th century by Franco (of Paris?)—the "Ars cantus mensurabilis"—as "the first and altogether one of the very greatest of the fundamental laws governing dissonance treatment." In modern terms, this law states in substance that at the beginning of

---

[13] See Riemann, *op. cit.*, pp. 112 ff. (for a detailed discussion) and Jeppesen, *op. cit.*, pp. 88 ff.

[14] "De musica mensurabili positio," Couss. *Script.*, 1: 104 ff. (Riemann, *op. cit.*, p. 116).

[15] *Ars cantus mensurabilis*, cap. 11 (see Riemann, *op. cit.*, p. 116); see also Shirlaw, *op. cit.*, p. 1.

[16] Franco of Cologne; Couss. *Script.*, 1: 154; see Riemann, *op. cit.*, p. 118; Shirlaw, *op. cit.*, p. 2.

[17] "in ordine ad diapason." [18] *Op. cit.*, pp. 90 ff. [19] Riemann, *op. cit.*, p. 135; Gerbert *Script.*, 3: 80 ff. [20] *Op. cit.*, p. 89.

each measure there shall be a consonance.[21] According to Jeppesen this law, while by no means fully observed in the succeeding centuries, continued to exert an influence, reaching, in Palestrina, the climax of its power. It is interesting to note that in Franco's own classification the fourth is a consonance and the sixth a dissonance; in the application of his own rule, therefore, the fourth would be permissible on the accent and the sixth not.

Tunstede (1351), according to Riemann,[22] a hundred years later includes the fourth and minor sixth with the imperfect dissonances, the major sixth, however, with the imperfect consonances.

Before this, however, evidences of a changing point of view are to be found in the treatise Anonymous XIII, which Riemann considers as being still in the 13th century. In this treatise the sixths are classed as imperfect consonances and the fourths as dissonances.[23] The date of the manuscript, however, is uncertain: it may belong in the 14th century.

Of music in more than two parts, which are necessary for a consideration of the six-four combination, the theorists of the 13th and 14th centuries write with a certain indecision, so that it is difficult to find anything like a direct reference to such a phenomenon. Principles of procedure were developing, however, in the fauxbourdon and in the Continental theories of three- or more-voiced music; and as has already been indicated in the consideration of the music itself, the 15th century shows a relatively advanced stage, from a modern viewpoint, in the solution of the various problems.

The beginning of the 14th century sees the gradual abandonment of the earlier names: Organum, Diaphonia, and Discantus, and the rise of the new term Contrapunctus, in connection with the "Ars nova." The sixth is definitely placed among the consonants and the fourth is omitted from the list of notes available for "Nota contra Notam" (note against note) use.[24] The *Ars discantus*, by Joh. de Muris,[25] contains a passage in which, in accordance with these views, the combination producing a six-four relation is specifically rejected.

Prodocimus de Beldemandis[26] in the beginning of the 15th century calls the thirds and sixths consonances and the fourth a dissonance although less than all the other dissonances, so that it takes a sort of intermediate position, and he remarks upon the fact that the ancients placed it among the consonants. He states further that dissonances may be used in figurated counterpoint where the dissonances are not felt because of the speed with which the voices move.[27]

---

[21] ". . . . in omnibus modis utendum est semper concordantiis in principio perfectionis, licet sit longa, brevis vel semibrevis."—Gerbert *Script.*, 3: 13.

[22] *Op. cit.*, p. 118.

[23] Couss. *Script.*, 3: 495; the same in Riemann, *op. cit.*, p. 123, "Encore est a savoir que de ces XIII espèces devant dites sont fais XIII acors, III parfais et IIII imparfais et VI dissonans. Les III parfais sont: unisson, quinte et double. Les IIII imparfais sont II tierces et II sixtes. Les VI dissonans sont II secondes, II quartes et II septimes . . . . ."

[24] Johannes de Garlandia; see Riemann, *op. cit.*, p. 239. The minor sixth alone was still occasionally omitted from the list of consonants; see *Ars contrapuncti secundum*, J. de Muris; Couss. *Script.*, 3: 59-60; Riemann, *op. cit.*, p. 253; see further Riemann, *op. cit.*, pp. 255-259.

[25] Couss. *Script.*, 3: 92 ff.; Riemann, *op. cit.*, p. 263, "4. Hat der Diskant die obere Sexte, so erhält der Contratenor die untere Terz, Quint (die hier am besten klingt), Oktave oder Dezime, aber nicht die Sexte."

[26] Couss. *Script.*, 3: 195; Riemann, *op. cit.*, p. 267, "Scias tamen quod quarto et sibi aequivalentes minus dissonant quam aliae combinationes dissonantes imo quodammodo medium tenent inter consonantias veras et dissonantias, in tantum quod, secundum quod quidam dicunt, ab antiquis inter consonantias numerabantur."

[27] Couss. *Script.*, 3: 197; Riemann, *op. cit.*, p. 268, "Usitandum tamen in cantu fractibili, eo quod in ipso propter velocitatem vocum earum non sentiuntur dissonantiae."

Although the syncope had previously been mentioned, Guilelmus Monachus (*ca.* 1450) is commonly credited with being the first theorist to explain its use except that he does not specifically speak of preparation.[28] Jeppesen and Riemann have both emphasized the importance of this step, the former pointing out the great psychological importance of the motive underlying the syncope dissonance, i.e., of "adding sweetness to the succeeding consonance,"—a conscious aesthetic motive; while the latter designates it as the first step toward a "normale Behandlung der Dissonanzen" (regular treatment of the dissonances).

As far as the evolution of the six-four chord is concerned, the adoption of the syncope dissonance by the theorists gave a theoretical justification for the use of such a combination in a more prominent way and this of course, in turn, promoted the conception of the phenomenon as a chordal entity. The close of the 15th century brings such theorists as Johannes Tinctoris, Adam von Fulda, Franchinus Gafurius, and many others who continued to develop and refine the concepts of dissonance treatment and to lay the foundations through their work for the growth of the harmonic viewpoint. Gafurius[29] speaks of the consonant fourth in a fauxbourdon passage as acceptable but in the next chapter forbids the free entrance of the six-four chord because the dissonance of the fourth in the lower position is not covered ("iccirco in gravibus ipsi sonis quartae hujusmodi discordiam contrapunctus non sustinet").

It is interesting and significant that, in the table of normal closes or cadences which Riemann quotes from Pietro Aron,[30] although the fourth syncope figures in seven of the nine examples, in no case does the sixth accompany it; evidence that as yet (early 16th century), even though it was not uncommonly found in the music of the period, the theorists did not recommend the six-four in the cadence formula. Riemann[31] points out that in all the examples of Aron none is given with the fifth of a chord in the bass (six-four chord) and few with the third, and he states further that "the *Toscanello* proves, that in 1523 Theory also really began to grasp the meaning of the triad and further that Practice had reached this point almost a hundred years earlier." Vicentino,[32] considering the intervals solely on their own merit or lack of merit, declared the sixths to be more dissonant than consonant but realized, however, their value in the context.

"Joseffo Zarlino" (1517-1590), says Riemann,[33] "stands like Seb. Bach on the border between two epochs, tersely summing up the knowledge of the one (the older) and at the same time brightly lighting the way to the other (the new)." There has been much discussion as to just how much of the modern viewpoint he really had. Ambros[34] is of the opinion that, although chords were known and rightly used, there was no real teaching of chords; that there was no concept of an inner relation between tone groups

$$\text{such as } \begin{matrix} g\ \acute{c}\ \acute{e} \\ e\ g\ \acute{c} \\ c\ e\ g \end{matrix} \text{; or in any event the emphasis was placed in the wrong place in that the}$$

---

[28] Jeppesen, *op. cit.*, pp. 205 ff.; Riemann, *op. cit.*, pp. 285 ff.

[29] *Practica musicae* (1495), 3, cap. 5; Riemann, *op. cit.*, pp. 334 f.

[30] *Toscanello in musica* (1523), 2, cap. 18; see Riemann, *op. cit.*, p. 345.

[31] *Op. cit.*, p. 348.

[32] *L'antica musica ridotta alla moderna* (Roma, 1555); see Riemann, *op. cit.*, p. 360.

[33] *Op. cit.*, p. 381; compare also Amb., 4: 415, and Shirlaw, *op. cit.*, p. 57.

[34] *Op. cit.*, p. 421.

intervals alone were considered. For example, Zarlino (according to Ambros), in considering the six-three and six-four chords ♮ pointed out the fourth as the common element, not the derivation by inversion from a common chord, "which even Zarlino's penetration does not notice at all." Zarlino[35] considers that the fourth accompanied by the minor third below sounds excellent—not so good accompanied by the major third, whereas the reverse is true when the third is placed above the fourth:

Harm. III, cap. 60        Zarlino Istit.

Buona    non buona      Buona    non buona

Riemann[36] believes that with the appearance (1571) of the "Dimostrazioni harmoniche" the last doubt disappears that Zarlino had a perfectly clear notion of the identity of chord combinations which differ only in the inversion, i.e., that he understood the principle of chord inversion.

Shirlaw,[37] however, is of the opinion that Riemann "reads into Zarlino's language what it certainly does not contain, and gives a wrong impression both as to what Zarlino has actually said, and as to what he actually means," and gives a lengthy refutation of Riemann's assertions. In summarizing his discussion he writes[38] as follows: ". . . . we find that Zarlino is acquainted with the principle of Octave inversion, but does not explain any of the intervals as rising from this principle; while of inverted chords he knows nothing. . . . ." Shirlaw further supports the latter view by pointing out that, although Zarlino considers the five-three chord the most perfect harmony (harmonia perfetta), he admits that many composers put the sixth in place of the fifth and that he not only permits but even recommends the substitution of the sixth for the fifth.[39]

Shirlaw does say, however (op. cit., p. 41), that Zarlino is quite familiar with the inversion of intervals and that he even demonstrates that the inverted interval has something in common with the interval of which it is the inversion, and further (p. 43) that ". . . . there is little question but that Zarlino, and other composers of and before his time, were quite well aware of the resemblance in harmonic effect existing between the harmony –c–e–g and the harmony e–g–ć–." If this is true then it would seem that Zarlino did have after all at least an inkling of a conception of chord inversion.

Zarlino's derivation of all the consonances from the numerical relation 1:2:3:4:5:6[40] places the fourth quite definitely among the consonances, yet, in actual practice above the bass, he considers it, just as the other theorists and composers have done, as a dissonance so that it may not occur on an accent except as a suspension.[41]

---

[35] Ist. Harm, 3, cap. 60.     [36] Op. cit., p. 372.     [37] Op. cit., p. 51.     [38] Op. cit., p. 53.

[39] Zarlino, Ist. Harm., 3, cap. 59, "È ben vero, che molte volte i Prattici pongono la Sesta in luogo della Quinta, & è ben fatto."

[40] Riemann, op. cit., p. 370, Zarlino, Ist. Harm., cap. 5, "Delle proprietà del numero Senario et delle sue parti et come tra loro so ritrova la forma d'ogni consonanze musicale."

[41] Zarlino, Dim. Harm., "Ragionamento Seconda," Def. X; compare Shirlaw, op. cit., p. 43.

Zarlino (Torchi) I, 71,2,1.

Compare Torchi I, 75,3,+2; and 76,2,1.

Thus, according to Zarlino, the six-four chord, as a dissonant combination, could occur only as an incidental phenomenon, as a "foil to the consonant harmonies," as Riemann so aptly expresses it.[42]

René Descartes[43] derives the fourth from the fifth, in that every time the fifth is heard the fourth is present "per accidens" (between the fifth and the upper octave which is also always present) and says that the reason why the fourth displeases is that it is the "shadow" not the substance and further calls it "infelicissima consonantiarum omnium." The minor sixth is mentioned as the octave complement of the major third but is not explained as derived from it as Shirlaw[44] points out "possibly for the reason that he would be unable to explain, in the same way, the major sixth as derived from the minor third seeing that the minor third is itself a derived interval." The major and minor sixths are explained as composite intervals arising from the combination of the major and minor thirds, respectively, with the fourth.

In the period of the *Generalbass* (chiefly during the 17th century) the concept of the triad and its inversions was gradually finding expression in clearer and clearer form in the writings of the theorists. Praetorius (1571-1621), Joh. Lippius (1609-1610), G. B. Doni (d. 1647), Mersenne (1636), Heinrich Albert (1643), Werkmeister (1698), Heinichen (1711), and Gottfried Keller (1701) who cites the six-four cadence as one of the three full closes,[45] may be mentioned in passing. Jean Philippe Rameau (1683-1764), however, is commonly credited as the actual founder of the modern theory of harmony. The use of the six-four chord in its various forms, as has already been seen, was an established factor in the works of composers more than a hundred years earlier. Here, as in so many other instances, practice precedes theory.

[42] *Ist. Harm.*, 3, cap. 27; Riemann, *op. cit.*, p. 384, "Che le Compositioni si debbono comporre primieramente di Consonanze et dopoi per accidente di Dissonanze. Et benche ogni Compositione et ogni Contrapunto et per dirlo in una sola parola ogni Harmonia si componi di Consonanze principalmente et primieramente . . . . la Dissonanza fa parer la Consonanza, la quale immediatamente la segue piu dilettevola."

[43] *Compendium musicae* (1618), cap. "de octava" and "de quarte"; compare Riemann, *op. cit.*, p. 378 and Shirlaw, *op. cit.*, p. 58.

[44] *Op. cit.*, p. 60.

[45] See Riemann, *op. cit.*, p. 428.

# CONCLUSION

T HE EVOLUTION of the six-four chord affords a valuable commentary upon the way in which the art of music developed during a most significant formative period. It shows how an apparently unimportant idiom or formula may become so crystallized in the minds of musicians, that in the course of time it exerts a directive influence on the progress of the art. This evolutionary process may be summarized by tracing the treatment of the different types of six-four chord through the several periods examined in the present research. Inasmuch as the name of the type suggests the treatment in each case, the chief points to be considered here are *relative frequency of occurrence* and *relation to the cadence formula*.

The accented (or semi-accented) six-four chord in which the fourth is prepared, type 1*a*, rarely occurs in the 13th- and 14th-century music and one must conclude that there is little indication of a particular use in relation to the cadence. In the First Netherland School it appears much more frequently; usually on the second degree of the scale in relation to the cadence, with the sixth sustaining while the fourth resolves to the third in the next chord $\left(\substack{6-\\43}\right)$. Several examples in which the sixth moves to the fifth as the fourth resolves to the third —$\substack{65\\43}$— have been found, but it is important to note that at this stage in the evolution of the six-four chord the formula occurs more often on the second degree of the scale than on the fifth. These combinations also occur occasionally on other degrees of the scale.

In the Second Netherland School the situation remains roughly the same with perhaps a slight tendency toward the restriction of the $\substack{6-\\43}$ to the second degree of the scale and of the $\substack{65\\43}$ to the fifth. The Third Netherland School, however, shows a decided preference for the use of the accented, prepared six-four chord in the $\substack{65\\43}$ formula on the fifth degree in a cadence. The other treatments of the earlier periods continue to appear, but much less often. From this time on the accented, prepared six-four is definitely established in the praxis as suitable cadence material. Although, in the periods under consideration, this chord is never used to any great extent in the final cadences at the end of movements and the like, chiefly for rhythmical reasons, it is very common in all sorts of intermediate cadences, modulations, etc. As a matter of fact, the cadential effect of the $\substack{65\\43}$ seems to have become so strong that when the formula occurs on the sixth, fourth, or other degree of the scale, as it not infrequently does, one of two things may be observed: either the note values are shortened so as to lessen the usual cadential effect, or there is a definite tendency to modulate to a nearly related key.

The accented (or semi-accented) six-four chord in which the fourth is not prepared, type 1*b*, is relatively common in the 13th and 14th centuries but with almost no suggestion of a definite relation to the cadence formula. In the 15th century several examples of the use of this chord on the fifth degree of the scale have been found, but in the periods following, with the increasing refinement in the treatment of the dissonance in general, this type of the six-four chord falls into disuse and does not appear again until its use in the works of Monteverdi and other composers outside the Palestrina school. Even in Monteverdi and the English madrigalists, the use of this type of the six-four chord is only relatively common, and the fourth may usually be analyzed as an accented passing note or an appoggiatura.

The auxiliary six-four, type 2$a$, is the most common type in the 13th and 14th centuries. There is little suggestion of other than merely incidental relation to a cadence formula. From the 15th century on, however, as has been pointed out in the various chapters of the present work, the auxiliary six-four becomes an integral part of certain cadence formulae and is to be found with increasing frequency in such relationships throughout the periods considered. In the 15th century the most common formula is $\frac{76\text{-}5}{4\text{-}3\text{-}}$, with minor variations, used principally on the second degree of the scale in the cadence. From the beginning of the 16th century the formula $\frac{65\text{-}}{4\text{-}3}$ increases in popularity until by the end of the century it is by far the most common of all the cadence formulae which involve the use of the six-four chord. In fact, this form becomes so stereotyped that in the hands of such composers as Monteverdi it serves as the point of departure into hitherto unexplored fields of dissonance treatment. The important result for all the future development of music is the crystallization of the concept of what are now known as the "dominant dissonances," the dominant seventh and ninth chords together with certain other derivatives.

The passing six-four, type 2$b$, has been discovered in all the periods examined. A careful study of the examples cited will reveal the fact that, while in a sense the least essential of the six-four chords, having its origin in the use of notes which in themselves are treated as some type of unessential material, the passing six-four chord makes an obvious and important contribution to the conception of a functional relationship between chords. By this is meant that, for example, when the passing six-four occurs on the second degree of the scale followed by the tonic triad, a certain similarity in effect is felt between this progression and the ordinary dominant-tonic progression when the bass moves from the fifth to the first degree of the scale. This idea of functional similarity is undoubtedly the soundest and most convincing argument for the classification of the six-four chord as the second inversion of a five-three chord. It is just this difference in function that has led many outstanding theorists to class the cadential six-four, not as a second inversion of a tonic chord, but simply as a decoration of a dominant chord.

Clear-cut examples of the arpeggio six-four, type 2$c$, are rare in the vocal music of the periods studied. In the instrumental music, however, they have been found in abundance from the end of the 16th century on. These chords show no particular relation to the cadence. They arise when the bass moves from one note to the other of the same chord. In other words, the bass simply moves in any one of a number of different ways to or from the fifth of the original triad without creating the impression of a chord change. Here the idea of the six-four chord as the second inversion of a triad finds its expression in an extremely natural and logical manner. In such situations the function of the three possible combinations, i.e., the five-three, six-three, and six-four positions, obviously remains the same, and for this reason it seems inevitable that they should simply be called different positions of the same chord. Under these conditions the six-four chord makes its nearest approach to being a consonant chord, at least so far as the treatment of the bass is concerned.

The thesis that the six-four chord at any moment in the periods studied, is treated as a purely consonant combination cannot successfully be defended. On the contrary, all the examples cited give overwhelming proof that the six-four chord is treated exclusively as a dissonance.[1] The freer uses of the fourth in the 15th and again in the early 17th century are entirely in accordance with the principles of dissonance treatment in the respective periods. Even in the 15th century, when the fourth enters freely, it commonly resolves quite regularly and in Monteverdi, with all his free resolutions, the fourth is usually prepared in the conventional way. At no time does one find both free entrance and free quitting of the six-four chord, i.e., the six-four both approached and quitted by a skip-wise progression of all the parts. The possibility of such a free treatment is of course an essential characteristic of the entirely consonant chords. In the periods under consideration only the five-three and six-three combinations are available for such a use and in this sense they constitute the only "essential" harmonic materials of these times.

The question just how far the idea of chord inversion was consciously developed, cannot of course be categorically answered. A strong case can, however, be made in support of the assumption that the concept of the six-four chord as the second inversion of a triad was highly developed by the first half of the 17th century. Many of the arguments have been pointed out in the body of the present work. Two of the most significant of them in the evolution of such an idea may be mentioned:

1. The functional similarity in the cadence formula between such a progression as $\begin{smallmatrix} V-VII-I \\ 6\ \ 6 \\ 4 \end{smallmatrix}$ $\left( or\ \begin{smallmatrix} VII-V-I \\ 6\ \ 6 \\ 4 \end{smallmatrix} \right)$, which was so common in the 15th century, and the usual V–I cadence which predominated in the later periods; and

2. The obvious tonal relationship between the various positions of the triad in those situations in which the "arpeggio" six-four occurs.

Surely no teacher of classical strict counterpoint who claims to base his rules on the procedures of the masters can, after an examination of the examples cited in the present work, reasonably exclude the use of the six-four chord, under similar restrictions, from the musical vocabulary of his students.

In summing up the evolution of the various forms of the six-four chord as it has been traced in the foregoing chapters, we have journeyed from the beginnings of polyphonic music to the middle of the 17th century. As the simultaneous combination of three tones, a lowest tone and two others sounding at the intervals of the fourth and the sixth above, the six-four chord is as old as the oldest music in three or more parts. The earliest musical records show many occurrences of this combination, and in them most of the types of the later periods are foreshadowed. In its evolution from these early, entirely incidental uses to the well defined and purposeful uses of the late 16th and early 17th centuries the six-four chord is seen to have played a not inconsiderable part in manifold interrelated developments, of great import for the future of the art of music, such as: (a) the crystallization of the idea of chord inversion, (b) the gradual refinement in the use of the dissonance, (c) the establishment of solid cadence formulae, (d) the growth of the feeling for tonality, and finally, (e) the inception of the notion of modulation.

---

[1] The so-called "consonant fourth" is, as Jeppesen (op. cit., p. 214) has pointed out, strictly speaking a misnomer. In spite of certain consonant characteristics it is still treated as a dissonance resolving, eventually, to a third over a stationary bass.

# BIBLIOGRAPHY

### AND

## LIST OF ABBREVIATIONS

ABERT, H., "Antike," *in* Adler (*q. v.*), revised by K. Sachs. Cited as Adler-Abert-Sachs.

ADLER, GUIDO, *Handbuch der Musikgeschichte* (ed. 2; Berlin, 1930). Cited as Adler. (Authors of the sections are cited as Adler-Lach, Adler-Ludwig, etc.).

——————, *Studie zur Harmonie* (Wien, Carl Gerold's Sohn, 1881).

ALBRECHTSBERGER, J. G., *Sämtliche Schriften* (ed. 2; Wien, Haslinger, 1837).

AMBROS, A. W., *Geschichte der Musik* (ed. 2; Leipzig, Leukert, 1880-1882), vols. 1-5 (Bd. V, Beispielband, Hg. v. Kade). Cited as Amb.

*Archiv für Musikwissenschaft* (Hg. v. Seiffert, usw.; Leipzig, Breitkopf und Härtel, 1918—). Cited as AfMW.

ARNOLD, W. F., "Das Fundamentum organisandi von C. Paumann," Chrysander Jahrbuch (Leipzig, 1867), vol. 2.

AUBRY, P., *Cent Motets du XIIIᵉ Siècle* (Paris, Rouart-Lerolle, 1908), vols. 1-3. Cited as Aubry.

BELLERMANN, H., *Der Kontrapunkt* (ed. 3; Berlin, Springer, 1887). Cited as Bellermann.

——————, *Die Mensuralnoten und Taktzeichen des XV. und XVI. Jahrhunderts* (Berlin, Reimer, 1858).

BORREN, C. VAN DEN, *Dufay—Son Importance dans l'Evolution de la Musique au XVᵉ Siècle* (Bruxelles, Hayez, 1925).

CAPELLEN, G., "Der Quartsextakkord," SIMG, 3 (1901-1902).

CHRYSANDER, K. F. F., *Jahrbuch für Musikwissenschaft* (Leipzig, 1863 and 1867). Cited as Chrysander Jahrbuch.

COUSSEMAKER, C. E. H. DE, *Histoire de l'Harmonie au Moyen-âge* (Paris, Didron, 1852).

——————, *L'Art Harmonique aux XIIᵉ et XIIIᵉ Siècles* (Paris, Durand, 1865).

——————, *Scriptores de musica medii aevi* (Paris, Durand, 1864-1876), vols. 1-4. Cited as Couss., *Script.*

——————, *Oeuvres complètes du trouvère Adam de la Halle* (Paris, Durand, 1872).

*Denkmäler der Tonkunst in Oesterreich* (Trienter Codices, Wien, Universaledition, 1900, 1904, 1912, 1920), vols. 7, pt. 1; 11, pt. 1; 19, pt. 1; 27, pt. 1. Cited as DTÖ.

*Early English Harmony* (ed. by H. V. Hughes; London, Plain Song and Mediaeval Music Society, 1913), vol. 2. Cited as *E. E. Harm.*

EITNER, R., *Bibliographie der Musik-Sammelwerke des XVI. und XVII. Jahrhunderts* (Berlin, 1877).

——————, *Biographisch-bibliographisches Quellen-Lexikon der Musiker und Musikgelehrten der christlichen Zeitrechnung bis zur Mitte des 19. Jahrhunderts* (Leipzig, Breitkopf und Härtel, 1900-1904).

FELLERER, K. G., *Der Palestrinastil und seine Bedeutung in der vokalen Kirchenmusik des 18. Jahrhunderts* (Augsburg, Filser, 1929).

FELLOWES, E. H., *The English Madrigal Composers* (Oxford Univ. Press, 1921).

FICKER, R., "Primäre Klangformen," *Jahrbuch der Musikbibliothek Peters* (Leipzig, 1929).

FISCHER, W., "Zur Kennzeichnung der mehrstimmigen Setzweise um 1500," StzMW, 5 (Beihefte der DTÖ; Wien, Artaria und Co., Universaledition, 1918).

——————, "Instrumentalmusik von 1450–1600," *in* Adler (*q. v.*) Cited as Adler-Fischer.

FULLER-MAITLAND, J. A., and BARCLEY SQUIRE, W., *Fitzwilliam Virginal Book* (London, Novello, 1897).

Fux, J. J., *Gradus ad Parnassum* (German trans., L. Mizler; Leipzig, Mizler, 1742). Cited as *Gradus*-Mizler.

Gerbert, M., *Scriptores ecclesiastici de Musica sacra potissimum* (Typis San-Blasianis, 1784), vols. 1-3. Cited as Gerbert, *Script.*

Gibbons, O., *The English Madrigal School* (ed. 2, ed. by E. H. Fellowes; London, Stainer and Bell, 1921), vol. 5. Cited as Gibbons V.

Gombert, N. (*See* Maldéghem.) Cited as Gom.

Gombosi, O. J., *Jacob Obrecht* (Leipzig, Breitkopf und Härtel, 1925).

Grove, G., *Dictionary of Music and Musicians* (ed. 3, ed. by H. C. Colles; 1927/28), Essays on "Harmony," "Counterpoint," etc.

Haas, R., "Il ritorno d'Ulisse in patria," StzMW, 9 (Beiheft der DTÖ; Wien, Universaledition, 1922.)

————, *Die Musik des Barocks* (Potsdam, Akademische Verlagsgesellschaft Athenaion, 1928).

Haberl, F. X., *Wilhelm du Fay*, VjfMW, I.

Heuss, A., *Studie über die Instrumentalstücke des "Orfeo"* (Inaug. diss.; Leipzig, 1903).

Hitzmann, C. F., *Geschichte des verminderten Septimen-Akkordes* (Berlin, Guttentag, 1854).

Hughes, Dom Anselm, *Worcester Mediaeval Harmony of the 13th and 14th Centuries* (Nashdom Abbey, Plain Song and Mediaeval Music Society, 1928).

*Jahrbuch der Musikbibliotek Peters* (Hg. v. E. Vogel, etc.; Leipzig, 1895—). Cited as Jahrbuch Peters.

Jeppesen, K., *The Style of Palestrina and the Dissonance* (Oxford Univ. Press, 1927).

————, *Der Kopenhagener Chansonnier* (Kopenhagen, Levin & Munksgaard; Leipzig, Breitkopf und Härtel, 1927). Cited as Jeppesen.

Josquin des Près, *Wereldijke Werken* (Hg. v. A. Smijers, Leipzig, Alsbach; Amsterdam, Siegel, 1925). Cited as Jos. W.

————, *Motetten* (aforementioned edition, 1926). Cited as Jos. M.

Kalhäne, A., "Gliederung des Tonbereichs," Müller-Pouillet, *Lehrbuch der Physik* (Braunschweig, Friedr. Vieweg und Sohn, 1929), vol. 1, pt. 3, "Akustik."

Kinkeldey, O., *Orgel und Klavier in der Musik des 16. Jahrhunderts* (Leipzig, Breitkopf und Härtel, 1910). Cited as Kinkeldey.

Kitson, C. H., *The Art of Counterpoint* (ed. 2; Oxford Univ. Press, 1924).

————, *The Evolution of Harmony* (ed. 2; Oxford Univ. Press, 1924).

Körte, O., "Laute und Lautenmusik bis zur Mitte des 16. Jahrhunderts," Beihefte der IMG, 3 (Leipzig, Breitkopf und Härtel, 1901).

Lach, R., *Studien zur Entwicklungsgeschichte der ornamentalen Melopöie* (Leipzig, Kahnt, 1913).

————, "Das Kadenz- und Klauselproblem in der vergleichenden Musikwissenschaft," *Zeitschrift für Oest. Gymnasien* (Wien, Hölder, 1916).

————, "Die Musik der Natur- und Orientalischen Kulturvölker," *in* Adler (*q.v.*). Cited as Adler-Lach.

Leichtentritt, H., "Claudio Monteverdi als Madrigalkomponist," SIMG, 11 (1909-1910).

————, *Geschichte der Motette* (Leipzig, Breitkopf und Härtel, 1908).

Louis, R., und Thuille, L., *Harmonielehre* (ed. 8; Stuttgart, Klett, 1913).

Ludwig, F., *Studien über die Geschichte der mehrstimmigen Musik im Mittelalter*, SIMG, 4,5,7.

————, "Die Musik des Mittelalters," *in* Adler (*q.v.*). Cited as Adler-Ludwig.

MacPherson, C., *A Short History of Harmony* (London, Kegan Paul, Trench, Trubner, and Co.)

Maldéghem, R. J. van, *Trésor Musical*. Collection authentique de musique sacré et profane des anciens maîtres belges (Bruxelles, Muquardt, 1865-93 [R = Religieuse, P = Profane]). Cited as T. M. 1866 R. or P., etc.

Malipiero, G. F., See Monteverdi.

*Monatshefte für Musikgeschichte* (Hg. v. der Gesellschaft für Musikforschung, redigiert v. R. Eitner; Leipzig, Breitkopf und Härtel, 1869-1905). Cited as MfMG.

MONTEVERDI, C., *Gesamtausgabe* (Hg. v. G. F. Malipiero; Wien, Universaledition, 1926).

MORLEY, T., *The English Madrigal School* (ed. by E. H. Fellowes; London, Stainer and Bell, 1913-), vols. 1-4. Cited as Morley I-IV.

MORRIS, R. O., *Contrapuntal Technique in the Sixteenth Century* (Oxford Univ. Press, 1922).

MÜNNICH, R., "Konkordanz und Diskordanz," ZIMG, 13.

OCKEGHEM, J., *Sämtliche Werke* (Hg. v. D. Plamenac; Leipzig, Breitkopf und Härtel, 1927). Cited as O.

OREL, A., "Einige Grundformen der Motettenkomposition im XV. Jahrhundert," StzMW, 7. (Beiheft der DTÖ; Wien, Universaledition, 1920).

————, "Katholische Kirchenmusik seit 1430," *in* Adler (*q.v.*). Cited as Adler-Orel.

*Oxford History of Music* (Oxford Univ. Press, 1901-1905), vols. 1 and 2. (Vol. 1, ed. 2, 1929.)

PAESLER, C., "Fundamentalbuch von Hans v. Constanz," VjfMW, 5.

PALESTRINA, G. P., *Gesamtausgabe* (Leipzig, Breitkopf und Härtel, 1862-1903). Cited as P.

PLAMENAC, D., "J. Ockeghem als Motetten- und Chansonkomponist" (Diss.; Wien, 1925).

POSPISCHIL, HEDWIG, "Untersuchungen über die psychologischen Wirkungen der Lagenverhältnisse" (Diss.; Wien, 1928).

*Proceedings* of the Musical Association (London, Novello, 1874—).

PRUNIÈRES, H., *Cl. Monteverdi* (Paris, Alcan, 1924).

————, *La Vie et l'Oeuvre de C. Monteverdi* (Paris, Libraire de France, 1926).

RIEMANN, H., *Geschichte der Musiktheorie* (Leipzig, Hesse, 1898; ed. 2, 1920).

————, *Handbuch der Musikgeschichte* (rev. ed. 2; Leipzig, Breitkopf und Härtel, 1919/20), vols. 1 and 2.

————, *Musiklexikon* (ed. 11; Berlin, Hesse, 1929).

RISCHBIETER, W., *Drei theoretische Abhandlungen über Modulation, Quartsextakkord und Orgelpunkt* (Dresden, Ries, 1879).

SACHS, CURT. *See* Abert.

*Sammelbände der internationalen Musikgesellschaft* (Hg. v. O. Fleischer und J. Wolf; Leipzig, Breitkopf und Härtel, 1899-1904). Cited as SIMG.

SCHAEFER, K. L., *Musikalische Akustik* (ed. 2; Berlin, Gruyter, 1923).

SCHERING, A., *Geschichte der Musik in Beispielen* (Leipzig, Breitkopf und Härtel, 1931). Cited as Schering.

SCHNEIDER, L., *Cl. Monteverdi* (Paris, Perrin, 1920).

SCHNEIDER, M., *Die Anfänge des Basso continuo und seiner Bezifferung* (Leipzig, Breitkopf und Härtel, 1918).

SHIRLAW, M., *The Theory of Harmony* (London, Novello, 1917).

SCHÖNBERG, A., *Harmonielehre* (ed. 3; Wien, Universaledition, 1922).

STAINER, J., *Dufay and His Contemporaries* (London, Novello, 1898). Cited as Stainer.

"Studien zur Musikwissenschaft" (Beihefte der DTÖ unter Leitung v. G. Adler; Wien, Universaledition). Cited as StzMW.

STÖHR, R., *Harmonielehre* (ed. 16; Wien, Universaledition, 1909).

TORCHI, L., *L'Arte Musicale in Italia* (Milan, Ricordi, 1897—), vols. 1 and 3.

*Tudor Church Music* (ed. by Terry, etc.; Oxford Univ. Press, since 1923), octavo ed. Nos. 1-50. Cited as TCM.

*Vierteljahrschrift für Musikwissenschaft* (Hg. v. Chrysander, etc.; Leipzig, Breitkopf und Härtel, 1885-1894). Cited as VjfMW.

VOGEL, E., "Claudio Monteverdi," VjfMW, 3.

WAGNER, P., *Geschichte der Messe* (Leipzig, Breitkopf und Härtel, 1913).

————, "Das Madrigal und Palestrina," VjfMW, 8.

WASIELEWSKI, J., *Geschichte der Instrumentalmusik im XVI. Jahrhundert* (Berlin, Guttentag, 1878).

WERNER, T. W., "Die Magnificat-Kompositionen A. Rener's," AfMW, 2:195.

WILBYE, J., *The English Madrigal School* (ed. by. E. H. Fellowes; London, Stainer and Bell, 1914), vol. 6. Cited as Wilbye VI.

WINTERFELD, C., *Johann Gabrieli und seine Zeit* (Berlin, Schlesinger, 1834).

WOLF, J., *Geschichte der Mensuralnotation von 1250-1460* (Leipzig, Breitkopf und Härtel, 1904), 3 vols. Cited as Wolf I, etc.

WOOLDRIDGE, H. E., "The Polyphonic Period," in *Oxford History of Music.*

ZARLINO, G., *Istituzioni Harmoniche* (Venetia, 1558), "Tutte l'Opera . . . ." (Venetia, 1589), vol. 1. Cited as *Ist. Harm.*

_____, *Dimostrazione Harmoniche* (Venetia, 1571), "Tutte l'Opera . . . ." (Venetia, 1589), vol. 2. Cited as *Dim. Harm.*

*Zeitschrift für Musikwissenschaft* (Leipzig, Breitkopf und Härtel, since 1918). Cited as ZfMW.

*Zeitschrift der internationalen Musikgesellschaft* (Leipzig, Breitkopf und Härtel, 1899-1914). Cited as ZIMG.

ZIEHN, B., *Harmonie- und Modulationslehre* (Berlin, Sulzer, 1887).

_____, *Manual of Harmony* (Milwaukee, Kaun, 1907).

# INDEX